CHORAL MUSIC
BY
AFRO-AMERICAN
COMPOSERS

A selected, annotated
bibliography
compiled by

EVELYN DAVIDSON WHITE

The Scarecrow Press, Inc.
Metuchen, N.J., & London
1981

Library of Congress Cataloging in Publication Data

White, Evelyn Davidson.
    Choral music by Afro-American composers.

    Discography: p.
    Includes index.
    1. Choruses--Bibliography. 2. Afro-Americans--
Music--Bibliography. I. Title.
ML128.C48W5   016.7841   81-8867
ISBN 0-8108-1451-X   AACR2

DEDICATION

TO MY DEVOTED HUSBAND, JAMES PATRICK WHITE;
TO THE MEMORY OF MY LATE SISTER, MARY
DAVIDSON ROBINSON; AND TO JAMES THOMAS
HOLLIDAY.

ACKNOWLEDGMENTS

The first survey of published choral music by Afro-American composers, completed by the author in 1975, was supported with a grant from the Faculty Research Program in Social Sciences, Humanities and Education at Howard University (Washington, D. C.). I am especially grateful to Dr. Lorraine Williams, Vice-President for Academic Affairs, for her continued interest, support, and concern.

I am deeply indebted to Dr. James T. Holliday of the music faculty of Howard University for his encouragement and invaluable assistance with research and other details involved in the project. I express my sincere gratitude to Sister Virginia Assumpta for the difficult task of typing the manuscript, and to Dr. Charles Walter Thomas, Sister Regina Therese, and Phyllis P. Goodman for valuable editorial assistance.

Grateful acknowledgment is made to those who served as consultants: Kenneth Billups of St. Louis, Arthur La Brew of Detroit, Dr. Vivian Flagg McBrier of Washington, D. C. , and Dr. Wendell Whalum of Atlanta.

Many colleagues and friends contributed to the preparation of this compilation by referring the author to composers and providing information about compositions by Afro-American composers. I express my sincere gratitude to these persons, whose names are too numerous to list.

I am deeply indebted to the personnel of the choral department of the Dale Music Company, Silver Spring, Md. , for their assistance and wonderful spirit of cooperation. Special thanks go to Emmy Moore, Gary Roper, and Dorothy Ferrara.

The most important contributions were made by composers and families of late composers who responded so generously to my requests for unpublished choral compositions and who gave their enthusiastic support and encouragement. To these persons I express my warmest appreciation and genuine gratitude.

iv

TABLE OF CONTENTS

CHORAL MUSIC BY AFRO-AMERICAN COMPOSERS:
A SELECTED, ANNOTATED BIBLIOGRAPHY

INTRODUCTION

Black composers have made substantial, noteworthy contributions to both the repertory of choral literature and the cultural heritage of America. Unfortunately, much of this literature, which represents all styles from simple four-part settings to avant-garde pieces, has not been performed because of the difficulty of locating many of these works and also because of a lack of interest. Conductors of singing ensembles should program with much greater frequency choral works representative of the styles of Afro-American composers so that the public will become better educated as to the quality, quantity, and rich variety of compositions and arrangements by Black composers. Throughout the country we have witnessed an unprecedented increase in choral activities on the part of public schools, colleges, churches, and communities.

> Of all the forms of musical expressions, choral singing is the most accessible to the amateur.... Because extensive and serious musical study is not an essential prerequisite for a satisfying choral experience, many children, teenagers, and adults throughout the world find delight and fulfillment as regular participants in this form of musical endeavor. It is the one art form that can provide for the nonprofessional a glimpse of transcendental beauty and musical self-fulfillment usually reserved for those who have devoted years of practice and study to their instruments. [1]

Opportunities for public performance of choral music are greater now than ever. Conductors should become more actively involved in helping the public to develop appreciation for choral music by Afro-American composers as well as for choral music representing a broad spectrum of styles and nationalities.

Special mention at this point should be made of choral conductors, now active, who have encouraged and promoted Black composers by regularly programming their art music as well as arrangements of spirituals. These conductors diligently search for music and attract the attention of Black composers, who frequently dedicate compositions to them and their choirs. Such a list would include the names of Kenneth Billups (St. Louis), Wendell Whalum (Morehouse College, Atlanta), Nathan Carter (Morgan State University, Baltimore), William Garcia (Talladega College, Talladega, Ala.), Carl G. Harris (Virginia State University, Petersburg), Noel Da Costa (New York City and Rutgers University), and Brazeal Dennard (Detroit). The author, who conducts the Evelyn White Chorale, regularly performs music by Black composers and has presented many programs devoted entirely to art music and spirituals of these composers, including a major performance at the National Gallery of Art in Washington, D. C., on December 1976.

My experience as conductor and clinician and my involvement as teacher of choral conducting for many years have made me acutely aware of the urgent need for properly annotated bibliographical materials that might serve as a useful tool for busy conductors who wish to perform music by Black composers. Because of the numerous requests I have received for information about these composers, and because of my deep conviction that their representative choral music must be heard and accepted as standard program literature, I have made a comprehensive survey of this music with the fervent hope that such a compilation will serve as an incentive to choral conductors to program little-known composers as well as familiar and unfamiliar works by established Black musicians. Especially does the Black choral conductor have an obligation to introduce to the public music of the highest quality as well as reasonably competent music representing the total spectrum of styles and compositional techniques of Black composers.   To fail to do so would be an abrogation of responsibility. The conductor is the critical link between the listener and composer, bringing to life the printed page of music.   The conductor's role is significant in the process of weaving music of quality and uniqueness by Afro-American composers into the total fabric of our music culture, where it quite properly belongs.

Although the classical music of Black composers has received an increasing amount of attention in recent years ... it still remains largely an unknown quantity to the public.   When references are made to the music of Black composers by the press and the media, it is generally assumed that such references are to blues, spirituals, gospel or jazz....   Only when this music is provided the opportunity to be heard can a valid judgement be made as to its worth and whether it should have a place in the concert repertory and in music history. [2]

Choral conductors frequently complain about the lack of source material and the limited samples of choral music by Black composers found in most retail music stores.   The purpose of this compilation is to supplement inadequate source materials about choral music of these composers and thereby encourage the performance of their music.   One has little difficulty locating works by composers who have made significant contributions to choral literature--among them such well-known names as William Dawson, R. Nathaniel Dett, Hall Johnson, Ulysses Kay, Undine Smith Moore, George Walker, and John Work III.   A more comprehensive list might well include the names of other highly gifted men and women: Leslie Adams, Noel Da Costa, Mark Fax, James Furman, Adolphus Hailstork, Robert Harris, Thomas H. Kerr, John Price, and Dorothy Rudd Moore, to mention only a few.

Most composers find it difficult to get their works published by major companies, and with the exception of a very small group that would include Ulysses Kay and Hale Smith, this is especially true of Black composers.   Several musicians were questioned about problems encountered in getting works performed, published, and recorded. [3] Some of their responses were as follows:

THOMAS JEFFERSON ANDERSON

"I am personally convinced that the availability of records, performances, commissions and publishers has little to do with musical worth. "

DAVID N. BAKER

"It is extremely difficult to get your works published or recorded. "

UNDINE SMITH MOORE

"The role of the black artist in this culture is not fully recognized.   It is as though he does not officially exist ... only a small percentage of what I have written has been published or recorded. "

HOWARD SWANSON

"I feel that the black creative artist has, to a great extent, been excluded from American history and the American cultural scene. "

The author examined several recommended lists of choral music and found dramatic illustrations of the extent to which the music of Afro-American composers has been neglected.   Two widely publicized books on choral conducting include lists of choral music.   In one book (1975) approximately 500 compositions are cited; 2 percent of the composers are Black.   Only the arrangements of spirituals by these composers are included; no art music is listed.   In the second book examined (1974) approximately 300 compositions are listed; only one was written by a Black composer.   The glaring omission of works by Afro-American composers is even more notable in the case of another popular list that includes approximately 1,200 titles of choral music.   The list of sacred and secular music includes one composition by a Black composer.   Approximately 90 spirituals are cited, and even in this category, only 15 are arranged by Black composers.

The quoted comments of recognized composers about the difficulty of publication and the instances of omission of names on popular lists of recommended choral music are incontrovertible examples of the neglect of Afro-American composers. Unfortunately, there is a yawning chasm between our desire to be accepted into the mainstream of the music culture of America and the actual accomplishment of this fact. These circumstances pose a steadily sharpening dilemma for Black composers and for Black America.

(Brief reference should be made here to compositions in manuscript that are included in this compilation. These works represent a rich treasury of choral music and in most cases are available upon request to the composer or surviving family member. The search for works of genuine quality among manuscripts can indeed be an exciting and rewarding venture. In many instances the best works of a composer are in manuscript because of the difficulty of publication.)

In a bibliography of choral works by Black composers it is not unexpected that a high percentage of compositions and arrangements would be based on thematic material from Afro-American spirituals and folksongs. Many of these arrangements are extended, elaborated forms--for example, "'Way Over in Beulah Lan'" and "Cert'n'ly Lord," by Hall Johnson; "Soon-Ah Will Be Done" and "There Is a Balm in Gilead," by William L. Dawson; "Po' Wayfaring Stranger" and "Talk About a Child," by Thomas H. Kerr, Jr. In these arrangements and many others included in this compilation the authenticity and uniqueness of the spirituals and folksongs are retained in the extended forms. R. Nathaniel Dett (1882-1943) was the first composer to use the theme of a spiritual as the "musical" idea on which an anthem ("Listen to the Lambs") is based. In discussing the anthem Dett stated:

> I recall that I wrote "Listen to the Lambs" out of a feeling that Negro people, especially the students of Hampton Institute, where I was then teaching, should have something musically which would be peculiarly their own and yet which would bear comparison with the nationalistic utterances of other peoples' work in art forms. [4]

Other composers have followed the example of Dett and have fused the elements of the spiritual with elements of the European style in settings and extended choral works.

Nevertheless, because of the policy of some publishers, Black composers have often complained that many of their works that are based on Afro-American folksong literature are not published. Hale Smith, a Black composer and music editor, has observed:

> More esoteric music might be published at times, but the odds are overwhelming that these works will sit on the shelves for years and make no money for anyone. Yet there is recognition that throughout the country there is rising pressure, especially in the school systems, for music relating to the Black experience. [5]

As to the purpose and scope of this bibliography, no attempt has been made to present an all-inclusive list of choral music by Afro-American composers, or to make judgments as to the quality of compositions included; the latter decision must be made by the conductor. While annotated sources are useful, they cannot substitute for the painstaking, time-consuming task of carefully examining, analyzing, and evaluating each choral work. Appropriateness and suitability of program selections must always be determined by the conductor with the capability and resources of a particular choir in mind.

Important sources used for this research project were the Moreland-Spingarn Collection at Howard University, Washington, D. C.; the Library of Congress; and the Azalia-Hackley Collection in Detroit. The extensive collection of the author and collections of other persons acknowledged earlier were also valuable sources of information. Catalogs of music publishing companies were examined as well as music in local stores.

Probably the most difficult phase of this project was that of locating unpublished music and music published by small companies. In this area of investigation composers were the chief sources of information.

The entries included in this bibliography are arranged by composer in alphabetical order, and eight items of information, as follows, are given for each:

a. copyright date (first copyright date only)
b. number of pages
c. voicing and solo requirements
d. vocal ranges
e. range of difficulty
f. a cappella; type of accompaniment
g. publisher
h. catalog number (if available)

The category "range of difficulty" may be open to criticism because it is the only subjective evaluation made for each entry and needs to be explained in some detail. This evaluation is made with the "average choir" in mind. The following characteristics have been used to define what may be assumed to be the average choir:

1. A few sight readers who quickly grasp new music, comprising at least 10 percent of the membership.

2. A high percentage of members who learn notes quickly even though they remain somewhat dependent on the sight readers.

3. Capabilities for hearing and listening to intervals, rhythmic patterns, harmony parts, and accompaniment.

4. Sufficient capability to handle reasonable ranges with ease.

5. Chorus sections that are strong enough to cope with their own musical assignments while help is being given to other parts.

6. An accompanist who is technically capable.

As Charles Burnsworth has noted,

No choir, of course, can rise above the technical capabilities and musical sensitivity of its conductor. The old adage that there are no bad choirs, only bad conductors is probably more true than is generally admitted. The standard of the average choir can be met or exceeded only to the extent of the conductor's musical endowments. [6]

The following elements were considered by the author in order to made a determination as to the range of difficulty for each entry:

a. Horizontal movement of each voice part
b. Intervallic relationships
c. Harmonic texture
d. Chromaticism
e. Vocal range
f. Dynamic range
g. Rhythmic complexity
h. Tempo
i. Frequency of modulations
j. Frequency of changing meters
k. Polytonality, atonality
l. Textual complexity
m. Type of accompaniment

The biographical sketches of Afro-American composers and arrangers included in this compilation reveal that approximately 50 percent at some point in their careers conducted college, high school, church, or community choirs.

Black college choirs and their directors have made significant contributions to our musical culture by presenting to audiences, most especially the Afro-American audiences, programs representing a broad spectrum of styles and generally including music by Afro-American composers and arrangers. Composers have often turned to college choirs for premiere performances of their work. Annual tours and concerts performed on college campuses have probably been the most important means of publicizing the contributions of Afro-American culture until recent years. Some of the best-known touring college groups, many of which still follow a tradition of excellence, have been Cotton Blossom Singers (Piney Woods, Miss.), Jubilee Singers (Fisk University, Nashville, Tenn.), Hampton Choir (Hampton, Va.), Howard University Choir (Washington, D. C.), Morehouse Choir (Atlanta), Talladega Choir (Talladega, Ala.), Tuskegee Institute Choir (Tuskegee, Ala.), and the Utica Jubilee Singers (Utica, Miss.).

Eileen Southern points out that the "new" generation of composers including Ulysses Kay, Thomas J. Anderson, Arthur Cunningham, George Walker, and Hale Smith won their reputations as composers "before becoming college professors.... There has been no pressure on them to write music specifically for performance by Black artists and groups."[7]

Carl G. Harris, Jr., has categorized the chief composers of choral music as follows:

Black Trailblazers: Harry Burleigh, John Wesley Work, Frederick J. Work, Robert Nathaniel Dett, Clarence White, James Weldon Johnson, J. Rosamond Johnson.

Black Nationalists: Hall Johnson, William Levi Dawson, John Wesley Work, III, Frederick Douglass Hall, and William Grant Still.

Black Innovators: Margaret Bonds, Ulysses Kay, Hale Smith, and Undine Smith Moore.[8]

Warner Lawson referred to the early group of composers as the "Afro-American Five":

If the "Russian Five" achieved success and recognition for their work in the folk idiom of their country, then five Negro composers, born after 1866, deserve the title of "Afro-American Five." These five include Henry Thackery Burleigh (1866-1949); Clarence Cameron White (1880-1960); R. Nathaniel Dett (1882-1943); William Grant Still (1895-1978) and William Levi Dawson (b. 1899). Covering a total span of 97 years, they bridge successfully the gap between raw folk music and concert music.... In large measure, the creative contribution of the "Afro-American Five" is as nationalistic as is the work of the "Russian Five." If their creative significance falls short of the Russians' achievement from a world point of view, this is understandable when one realizes the racial obstacles which yet, at that time, had to be overcome.[9]

Eileen Southern refers to most of the "post-slavery Black composers--i. e. those born before 1900" as nationalists in the sense that they turned to the folk music of their people.[10]

The young Black composers who emerged during the mid-century years were eclectic.... The one quality they shared in common was that each believed it important to chart his own course.... Some exploited more thoroughly the African tradition with its emphasis on functionalism, communication and purpose; others made the effort to combine African and European traditions into an integrated whole; a few ignored the problems and wrote wholly in the European tradition.[11]

With this generation of composers, and younger gifted composers including James Furman, Adolphus Hailstork, John Price, Robert Harris, Dorothy Rudd Moore, and many others, the creative activity of Afro-American composers has come to a notable peak, representing a growing diversity of styles and variety in the use of musical forces.

Notes

1. Ray Robinson. The Choral Experience. New York: Harper and Row, 1976, p. 3.

2. Dorothy Maxine Sims. "An Analysis and Comparison of Piano Sonatas by George Walker and Howard Swanson," The Black Perspective in Music, 4, 1 (Spring 1976), 70.

3. David N. Baker, Lida M. Belt, and Herman C. Hudson, eds. The Black Composer Speaks. Metuchen, N. J.: Scarecrow, 1978.

4. Vivian Flagg McBrier. R. Nathaniel Dett: His Life and Works. Washington, D. C.: Associated Publishers, 1977, p. 36.

5. Dominique-Rene de Lerma. Black Music in Our Culture. Kent, Ohio: Kent State University Press, 1970, p. 116.

6. Charles C. Burnsworth. Choral Music for Women's Voices. Metuchen, N. J.: Scarecrow, 1968, pp. 55-56.

7. Eileen Southern. "America's Black Composers of Classical Music," The Music Educator's Journal, 62, 3 (November 1975), pp. 46-59.

8. Carl G. Harris. "A Study of Characteristic Trends Found in Choral Works of a Selected Group of Afro-American Composers and Arrangers." D. M. A. dissertation, University of Missouri, Kansas City, 1972, pp. 9-32.

9. Warner Lawson. "American Negro Music and the American Negro Composer--1862-1962" (unpublished).

10. Eileen Southern. The Music of Black Americans. New York: Norton, 1971, p. 283.

11. Ibid., p. 462.

AFRO-AMERICAN COMPOSERS AND ARRANGERS

The following list of Afro-American composers and arrangers includes major contributors to choral literature as well as composers better known for compositions in other media: Thomas Jefferson Anderson, David N. Baker, Hale Smith, Carman Moore, Coleridge-Taylor Perkinson, and Howard Swanson.

1. Adams, Leslie
2. Anderson, Thomas Jefferson
3. Archer, Dudley Malcolm
4. Baker, David N.
5. Banks, Robert
6. Billups, Kenneth Brown
7. Boatner, Edward H.
8. Bonds, Margaret
9. Burleigh, Harry Thacker
10. Carter, Roland
11. Childs, John
12. Clark, Rogie Edgar
13. Clary, Salone Theodore
14. Coleman, Charles D.
15. Cooke, Charles L.
16. Cooper, William B.
17. Cunningham, Arthur
18. Curtis, Marvin
19. Da Costa, Noel George
20. Davis, Elmer L., Sr.
21. Dawson, William Levi
22. De Paur, Leonard
23. Dett, Robert Nathaniel
24. Diton, Carl R.
25. Duncan, John
26. Fax, Mark
27. Furman, James
28. Gillum, Ruth Helen
29. Gregory, Percy
30. Hailstork, Adolphus C., III
31. Hairston, Jacqueline Butler
32. Hairston, Jester
33. Hall, Frederick Douglass
34. Hancock, Eugene Wilson (White)
35. Handy, William Christopher
36. Harris, Robert A.
37. Hicks, Roy Edward
38. James, Willis Laurence
39. Jessye, Eva
40. Johnson, Hall
41. Johnson, J. Rosamond
42. Kay, Ulysses Simpson
43. Kerr, Thomas H., Jr.
44. King, Bettye Jackson
45. Logan, Wendell
46. McLin, Lena Johnson
47. Margetson, Edward Henry
48. Mayes, Robert
49. Mells, Herbert Franklin
50. Merrifield, Norman L.

51. Montague, J. Harold
52. Moore, Carman Leroy
53. Moore, Dorothy Rudd
54. Moore, Undine Smith
55. Nickerson, Camille
56. Parker, Reginald Nathaniel
57. Perkinson, Coleridge-Taylor
58. Perry, Julia Amanda
59. Pittman, Evelyn LaRue
60. Price, Florence B.
61. Price, John
62. Reece, Cortez D.
63. Rivers, Father Clarence Joseph
64. Roberts, Howard
65. Robinson, Alphonse
66. Robinson, Josephus
67. Roxbury, Ronald
68. Ryder, Noah Francis

69. Simpson, Eugene Thamon
70. Smith, Hale
71. Smith, William Henry
72. Southhall, Mitchell Bernard
73. Still, William Grant
74. Stor, Jean (pseud., William Astor Morgan)
75. Swanson, Howard
76. Taylor, Maude Cummings
77. Tillis, Frederick Charles
78. Walker, George Theophilus
79. Whalum, Wendell Phillips
80. White, Clarence Cameron
81. Williams, Arnold K.
82. Williams, Henry G.
83. Williams, Julius
84. Wilson, Olly
85. Work, John Wesley, III

KEY TO ABBREVIATIONS AND SYMBOLS

A	alto
ACA	American Composers Alliance
A Cap	a cappella
Asso	Associated Music Publishers
B	bass
Bar.	baritone
BH	Boosey and Hawkes
BR	Broadman Press
CA	Choral Arts
CF	Carl Fischer
CP	Choral Press
D	difficult (refers to range of difficulty)
DAN	Dangerfield Music Co.
D'LAN	D'Langer Music Co.
E	easy (refers to range of difficulty)
ECS	E. C. Schirmer Music Co.
FS	Fitzsimons Music Co.
GM	General Music Co.
GS	G. Schirmer Music Co.
GWM	General Words and Music
HL	Hal Leonard Music, Inc.
HM	Schmitt, Hall-McCreary
JC	John Church
JF	J. Fischer and Brothers
LC	Library of Congress (Washington, D. C.)
LG	Lawson-Gould
M	medium (refers to range of difficulty)
MCA	Music Corporation of America
MD	medium difficult (refers to range of difficulty)

Mez.	mezzo-soprano
MS	manuscript (copies in manuscript available from composer)
Nar.	narrator
ND	no date
NSMP	Northwestern School of Music Press
NV	New Valley Press
Orch.	orchestra
P	pages
PC	private collection
PLY	Plymouth Music Co.
PM	Piedmont Music Co.
Rich	Richmond Press
Rod	Rodeheaver-Hall Mark Co.
S; Sop.	soprano
Sch	Schuman Music Co.
Skid	Skidmore Music Publications
SSP	Slave Ship Press
T; Ten.	tenor
Volk	Volkein Brothers
WM	M. Witmark and Sons
WT	Weintraub Music Co.

SYMBOLS USED TO INDICATE VOCAL RANGES

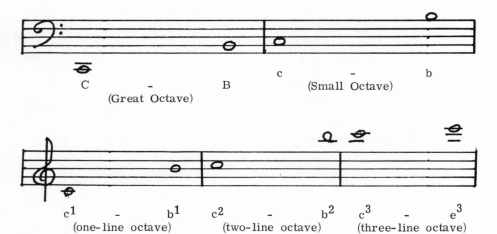

C   -   B   c   -   b
     (Great Octave)   (Small Octave)

c¹   -   b¹   c²   -   b²   c³   -   e³
(one-line octave)   (two-line octave)   (three-line octave)

ANNOTATED LIST
OF COMPOSITIONS

Composer or Arranger	Title; Copyright Date; Number of Pages	Voicing, Soloist	Vocal Range Women	Vocal Range Men	Range of Difficulty	A Cappella Accompaniment Instrumentation	Publisher	Catalog Number
ADAMS, Leslie	Hosanna to the Son of David; 1976; 15p	SATB	b^b – a^{b2}	A^b – g^{b1}	MD	Piano	Walton	2927
	Love Song; 1978; 12p	SATB	g – g^2	F – g^1	D	Piano	MS	
	Madrigal; 1973; 5p	SATB	g – $g^{\#2}$	G – g^1	MD	A Cap	MS	
	Psalm 121; n. d. ; 16p	SATB	f – a^{b2}	F – g^{b1}	D	A Cap	MS	
	Tall Tales; 1977; 12p	SATB	g^b – f^2	G – f^1	MD	Piano	MS	
	Under the Greenwood Tree; 1973; 4p	SATB	a – f^2	G^b – g^1	MD	A Cap	MS	
ANDERSON, T. J.	Personals (Cantata); 1966; 55p	SATB			MD	Brass ensemble	ACA	
	Spirituals; 1979; 83p	SATB/Ten.			D	Orch., jazz quartet, chorus, children's choir, nar.	ACA	
	This House; 1971; 35p	TTBB			D	4 chromatic pitch pipes	ACA	
ARCHER, Dudley	My Spirit on Thy Care; 1965; 5p	SATB	b^b – g^2	G – g^1	E	Organ	CF	CM7457
BAKER, David	Any Human to Another; n. d. ; 12p	SATB	a – a^2	F – f^1	M	Piano	MS	
	Five Songs to the Survival of Black Children; 1970; 19p	SATB			MD	A Cap	MS	
	I. Now That He Is Safely Dead		a – a^2	D^b – g^1				
	II. Religion		b^b – e^{b2}	F – f^1				
	III. Black Children		a^b – g^2	D – a^1				
	IV. The Dream Boogie		c^1 – g^2	F – f^1				

Composer or Arranger	Title; Copyright Date; Number of Pages	Voicing, Soloist	Vocal Range (Women)	Vocal Range (Men)	Range of Difficulty	A Cappella Accompaniment Instrumentation	Publisher	Catalog Number
BAKER (continued)	V. If We Must Die		$g - g^2$	$E - f^1$				
	I Dream a World; n.d.; 17p	SATB/Sop.	$ab - a^2$	$D - g^1$	MD	A Cap	MS	
	Psalm 23; 1972; 28p	SATB	$g - g^2$	$E - g^{b1}$	M	Organ	MS	
	Thou Dost Lay Me in Thy Dust of Death (from Black America); 1976; 4p	SATB	$a - f^2$	$E - f^1$	E	A Cap	Asso	A-129
BANKS, Robert	The Praise Chorale; 1972; 47p	SATB/Alto			M	Piano	Belwin	SB893
BILLUPS, Kenneth	Cain and Abel; 1967; 6p	SATB	$bb - g^2$	$A^b - e^{b1}$	E	Piano	CA	S-166
	Cert'ly Lord; 1950; 8p	SATB/Bass	$d^1 - g^2$	$c - e^1$	M	A Cap	Belwin	1047
	Everytime I Feel the Spirit; 1950; 8p	SATB	$bb - bb2$	$B^b - a^{b1}$	M	A Cap	Scholin	1040
	I Stood on the River of Jordan; 1950; 6p	SATB	$a - f^2$	$F - g^1$	M	A Cap	Scholin	1041
	I Want Jesus to Walk with Me; 1950; 6p	SATB	$c^1 - g^2$	$F - f^1$	M	Piano	Belwin	1048
	My Soul Is a Witness; 1950; 7p	SATB	$d^1 - bb2$	$B^b - g^1$	M	A Cap	Choral Press	1889
	New Born Again; 1951; 8p	SATB	$c^1 - a^2$	$F - a^{b1}$	M	A Cap	Belwin	1100
	Stand the Storm; 1967; 8p	SATB	$a - f^2$	$F - f^1$	M	Piano	CA	R-210
	Swing Low, Sweet Chariot; 1941; 11p	SATB/Sop.	$d^1 - e^2$	$G - e^1$	MD	A Cap	GS	8657
BOATNER, Edward	The Angel Rolled the Stone Away; 1954; 11p	SATB	$a - g^2$	$A - f^1$	M	A Cap	Colombo	NY1657
	Baby Bethlehem; 1964; 11p	SATB	$a - g^2$	$G - e^1$	E	A Cap	Colombo	NY2378

Composer or Arranger	Title; Copyright Date; Number of Pages	Voicing, Soloist	Vocal Range		Range of Difficulty	A Cappella Accompaniment Instrumentation	Publisher	Catalog Number
			Women	Men				
BOATNER (continued)	The Crucifixion; 1953; 6p	SATB/Sop.	g - f²	G - e¹	M	A Cap	Hammon	222
	Done Made My Vow; 1979; 7p	SATB/Ten.	b♭ - g²	G - f¹	M	Piano	McAfee	M1187
	Freedom Suite; 1966; 123p	SATB/Nar.			M	Orch.	MS	
	Go Tell It on the Mountain; 1979; 7p	SATB	c¹ - a♭2	A♭ - f¹	E	Piano	McAfee	M1188
	Hold On; 1979; 7p	SATB	b - g²	(E)G - f#1	E	Piano	McAfee	M1189
	I Want Jesus to Walk with Me; 1949; 7p	SATB	b♭ - a♭2	F - f¹	MD	A Cap	Galaxy	GMC1735
	In Bright Mansions; 1964; 9p	SATB	a - f²	A - f	E	A Cap	Colombo	NY2377
	I've Been 'Buked; 1979; 7p	SATB	b♭ - g²	G - e¹	E	Piano	McAfee	M1190
	Lord, I Can't Stay Away; 1952; 10p	SATB	a - a²	G - f#1	M	A Cap	Hammon	
	Man from Nazareth; 1971 Musical production depicting the life of Christ as interpreted by 25 spir-ituals arranged by Boatner	SATB					MS	
	Oh, What a Beautiful City; 1979; 8p	SSATBB	b - g²	G - g¹	M	Piano	McAfee	M1189
	On Ma Journey; 1956; 11p	SATB/Alto Ten.	b♭ - e♭2	A♭ - e♭1	M	A Cap	Colombo	NY1778
	Sinner Don't Let This Harvest Pass; 1952; 11 p	SATB	a - g²	G - g¹	M	A Cap	Hammon	
	Soon I Will Be Done; 1949; 11p	SATB	b♭ - a²	G - f¹	MD	A Cap (piano op.)	Colombo	NY1655
	The Star; 1964; 9p	SATB	a - f²	F - f¹	M	A Cap	Colombo	NY2379
	Trampin'; 1954; 8p	SATB	b - g²	G - e¹	M	A Cap	Galaxy	2019
	When I Get Home; 1954; 11p	SATB	b♭ - g²	A♭ - f¹	E	A Cap	Ricordi	NY1656

Composer or Arranger	Title; Copyright Date; Number of Pages	Voicing, Soloist	Vocal Range		Range of Difficulty	A Cappella Accompaniment Instrumentation	Publisher	Catalog Number
			Women	Men				
BOATNER (continued)	Who Is That Yonder?; 1954; 10p	SATB/Sop.	$c^1 - a^{b2}$	$F - f^1$	MD	A Cap (piano op.)	Colombo	FC1660
	You Hear the Lambs A-Crying; 1952; 10p	SATB/Ten.	$a - g^{b2}$	$B - b^{b1}$	M	A Cap	Ricordi	217
BONDS, Margaret	The Ballad of the Brown King; 1961; 56p (A Christmas Cantata)	SATB/Ten.			M	Piano	Fox	
	Children's Sleep; 1972; 5p	SATB	$a - e^2$	$E - f^{#1}$	M	Piano	CF	CM4715
	Ezek'el Saw the Wheel; 1959; 7p	SATB	$a - f^{#2}$ (a^2)	$A - f^{#1}$	E	Piano	Presser	312-40860
	Go Tell It on the Mountain; 1962; 6p	SATB	$c^1 - e^2$	$B - g^1$	E	A Cap	Mercury	MC432
	I Shall Pass Through This World; 1967; 7p	SATB	$c^1 - g^2$	$A - f^1$	M	A Cap	Bourne	829
	The Negro Speaks of Rivers; 1942; 12p	SATB	$a - d^2$	$G - f^1$	M	Piano	Handy	
	You Can Tell the World; 1946, 1964; 8p	TTBB		$F - f^1$ (a^1)	M	A Cap	Mutual	122
	You Can Tell the World; 1946, 1964; 8p	SSA	$a - a^2$		M	A Cap (guitar op.)	Mutual	121
BURLEIGH, Harry T.	Behold That Star; 1928; 11p	SATB	$c - g^2$	$F - f^1$	M	Organ	Ricordi	NY785
	Couldn't Hear Nobody Pray; 1922; 7p	SATB/Sop. Ten.	$a - f^2$	$F - a^1$	M	Piano	Ricordi	NY278
	De Creation; 1922; 2p	TTBB		$E^b - a^{b1}$	E	A Cap	Ricordi	NY229
	Deep River; 1913; 3p	SATB	$b - g^2$	$F^b - g^1$	E	A Cap	GS	5815
	Didn't My Lord Deliver Daniel?; 1916; 8p	SATB	$b^b - g^2$	$G - f^1$	M	A Cap	GS	6505

Composer or Arranger	Title; Copyright Date; Number of Pages	Voicing, Soloist	Vocal Range — Women	Vocal Range — Men	Range of Difficulty	A Cappella Accompaniment Instrumentation	Publisher	Catalog Number
BURLEIGH (continued)	Dig My Grave; 1913; 4p	SATB	$b^b - f^2$	$E^b - f^1$	E	A Cap	GS	5815
	Ethiopia's Paean of Exaltation; 1921; 15p	SATB	$c^1 - b^b2$	$F^b - g^b1$	M	Piano	Ricordi	NY107
	Everytime I Feel de Spirit; 1925; 11p	SATB/Alto Bar.	$a - f^2$	$F - f^1$	M	A Cap	Ricordi	FC488
	Ezekiel Saw de Wheel; 1927; 13p	SSA	$a(e) - a^2$		M	A Cap	Ricordi	NY699
	Ezekiel Saw de Wheel; 1927; 13p	SATB	$f - g^2$	$G - f^1$	M	A Cap	Ricordi	NY700
	Ezekiel Saw de Wheel; 1928; 11p	SATB	$d^b1 - e^b2$	$E^b - f^1$	M	A Cap	Ricordi	NY768
	A Fatuous Tragedy; 1928; 6p	TTBB		$E^b - a^b1$	M	A Cap	Ricordi	NY714
	Go Tell It on the Mountain; 1929; 8p	SATB	$a - g^2$	$G - e^1$	E	Organ	Ricordi	NY817
	De Gospel Train; 1927; 7p	SATB	$a - f^2$	$F - d^1$	E	Piano	Ricordi	NY659
	Hear de Lamb A-Cryin'; 1927; 12p	SATB/Alto Bar.	$c^1 - a^2$	$E - g^1$	M	A Cap	Belwin	NY658
	Heavn'n, Heav'n; 1921; 9p	SATB	$b^b - d^2$	$E^b - f^1$	M	Piano	Ricordi	NY122
	Ho, Ro, My Nut-Brown Maiden; 1930; 10p	TTBB		$F - a^1$	M	A Cap	Ricordi	NY847
	Hold On; 1938; 13p	SATB	$g - g^{\#}2$	$E - f^1$	M	A Cap	Ricordi	NY1113
	I Hope My Mother Will Be There; 1924; 5p	SATB	$c^1 - f^2$	$A^b - d^b1$	E	A Cap	Ricordi	NY414
	I've Been in de Storm So Long; 1944; 9p	SATB	$a - g^2$	$G - g^1$	M	A Cap	Ricordi	NY1310
	Little Mother of Mine; 1929; 11p	SATB	$c^1 - f^1(a^2)$	$F - g^1$	E	Piano	Ricordi	NY818
	Mister Banjo; 1924; 9p	SATB/Sop.	$e^1 - b^2$	$E - f^{\#}1$	M	A Cap	Ricordi	NY952
	My Lord, What a Mornin'; 1924; 7p	SATB	$b^b - a^2$	$E^b - f^1$	MD	A Cap	Belwin	FCC412

Composer or Arranger	Title; Copyright Date; Number of Pages	Voicing, Soloist	Vocal Range Women	Vocal Range Men	Range of Difficulty	A Cappella Accompaniment Instrumentation	Publisher	Catalog Number
BURLEIGH (continued)	Nobody Knows the Trouble I've Seen; 1924; 7p	SATB	b^b – $b2$	E^b – $a1$	M	A Cap	Belwin	FCC406
	O Lord Have Mercy on Me; 1935; 5p	SATB	b^b – $b2$	C – $b1$	E	A Cap	Ricordi	NY987
	O Southland; 1914; 7p	TTBB		E^b – $a1$	M	A Cap	Ricordi	116034
	O Southland; 1929; 7p	SATB	d^1 – g^2	G – g^1	MD	A Cap	Ricordi	NY1768
	The Promised Land; 1929; 8p	SATB/Mez.	b^b – $b2$	E^b – f^1	E	Piano	Ricordi	NY831
	Scandalize My Name; 1922; 2p	TTBB		E^b – g^1	E	A Cap	Ricordi	NY229
	Sometimes I Feel Like a Motherless Child; 1949; 5p	SSA	a – a^2		M	Piano	Ricordi	116543
	Southern Lullaby; 1920; 8p	SATB/Sop.	c^1 – f^2	A^b – g^1	E	A Cap	Ricordi	NY22
	Steal Away; 1924; 9p	SATB	b^b – g^2	G – $f^{\#1}$	M	A Cap	Ricordi	NY422
	'Tis Me, O Lord; 1924; 7p	TTBB		F – f^1 (bb1)	M	A Cap	Ricordi	NY424
	Wade in de Water; 1925; 9p	SATB	c^1 – $a2$	F – f^1	M	A Cap	Ricordi	NY487
	Walk Together Children; 1938; 5p	SSA or TTB	b – g^2	B – g^1	E	A Cap	Ricordi	NY1118
	Were You There?; 1927; 7p	SATB	b^b – $b2$	F^b – $b1$	M	A Cap	Ricordi	NY423
	Were You There?; 1927; 7p	SSA	g – $b2$		M	A Cap	Ricordi	NY693
	You Goin' to Reap Jus' What You Sow; 1938; 9p	SATB	a – g^2	F – f^1	M	A Cap	Ricordi	NY1134
CARTER, Roland	Five Choral Responses; 1978; 5p 1. Introit (Let the Heav'n Light Shine on Me) 2. Prayer Response (I'm Troubled)	SATB	b^b – $a2$	G – $f^{\#1}$	E	A Cap	Mar-vel	

Composer or Arranger	Title; Copyright Date; Number of Pages	Voicing, Soloist	Vocal Range Women	Vocal Range Men	Range of Difficulty	A Cappella Accompaniment Instrumentation	Publisher	Catalog Number
CARTER (continued)	3. Prayer Response (Come Here Jesus, If You Please)							
	4. Benediction (Lord, Make Me More Holy)							
	5. Sevenfold Amen							
	Give Me Jesus; 1979; 6p	SATB	$b^b - g^2$	$A^b - f^1$	E	A Cap	Mar-vel	
	I Want to Die Easy; 1978; 9p	SATB	$b - a^2$	$E - e^1$	E	A Cap	Mar-vel	
	Life Every Voice and Sing; 1978; 11p	SATB	$b - b^{b}2$	$B^b - f^1$	M	Piano	Mar-vel	
	Steal Away; 1979; 6p	SATB	$g - g^2$	$G - g^1$	E	A Cap	Mar-vel	
	You Must Have That True Religion; 1979; 8p	SATB/Sop.	$a - a^2$	$F - f^1$	M	A Cap	Mar-vel	
CHILDS, John	Alleluia; n.d.; 37p	SATB	$a^b - b^{b}2$	$A - b1$	D	Piano/percussion	MS	
	E Tenebris: Op. 7; 1965; 18p	SATB/Ten.	$b - a^2$	$A - a^1$	MD	Piano	MS	
	Music When Soft Voices Die; n. d.; 6p	SATB	$a - b^{b}2$	$D - a1$	MD	A Cap	MS	
	Tears; n. d.; 2p	SA	$a - f^{\#}2$		E	Piano	MS	
CLARK, Rogie	Earth Chant; n. d.; 11p	SATB	$c^1 - a^2$	$A - f^1$	M	Piano	PC	
	Let Us Cheer the Weary Traveler; 1925; 8p	SATB	$b - g^2$	$A - f^{\#}1$	M	A Cap	BH	5068
	Mango Walk; 1956; 11p	SATB	$g - g^2$	$A - e^1$	M	Piano	BH	5101
	The Old Ark; n. d.; 8p	SATB	$b^b - a^2$	$B^b - f^1$	M	A Cap	PC	
	Ride on King Jesus; 1951; 4p	SATB	$g - a^2$	$G - f^{\#}1$	M	A Cap	Kjos	5149
	Sit Down, Servant, Sit Down; 1955; 4p	SATB/Sop.	$g - a^2$	$E^b - f^1$	E	A Cap	BH	5067

Composer or Arranger	Title; Copyright Date; Number of Pages	Voicing, Soloist	Vocal Range Women	Vocal Range Men	Range of Difficulty	A Cappella Accompaniment Instrumentation	Publisher	Catalog Number
CLARK (continued)	Six African Folk Songs; 1975; 7p 1. Hey, Motswala 2. Kaffir Drinking Dance Song 3. Everybody Loves Saturday 4. The Proverbs 5. The Hare's Dance Song 6. Song of Farewell	SATB	$b^b - f^2$	$G - e^1$	M	A Cap/piano	PM	MC4624
	Six Afro-American Carols for Christmas; 1971; 7p 1. Christ Is Born 2. Creole Christmas Carol 3. Rise Up, Shepherd 4. The New Babe 5. Go Tell It on the Mountain 6. Mary Had a Baby	SATB	$a - g^2$	$G - f^1$	M	Piano	PM	4587
	Six More Afro-American Carols for Christmas; 1973; 7p 1. Sister Mary 2. O, Mary 3. Sing Christ Is Born 4. Song of Judea 5. Go Where I Send Thee 6. Angels, Ring Them Bells	SATB	$b^b - g^2$ (ab2)	$A^b - f^{\#1}$	E	Piano	PM	MC4600
	Six Afro-American Carols for Easter; 1972; 7p 1. Were You There? 2. One Sunday Morning 3. Calvary 4. They Led My Lord Away 5. The Crucifixion 6. He Rose from the Dead	SATB	$a - f^2$	$G - f^1$	M	Piano	PM	15622-6
	Soon-a Will Be Done; 1951; 8p	SATB	$a - f^{\#2}$	$B - f^{\#1}$	M	A Cap	Kjos	5148

Composer or Arranger	Title; Copyright Date; Number of Pages	Voicing, Soloist	Vocal Range — Women	Vocal Range — Men	Range of Difficulty	A Cappella Accompaniment Instrumentation	Publisher	Catalog Number
CLARK (continued)	There's a Man Goin' Roun'; 1940; 8p	SATB/Sop.	$b - b^2$	$G - g^1$	M	A Cap	Handy	
	This Wicked Race; n. d.; 9p	SATB	$b - g^2$	$G - e^1$	MD	A Cap	PC	
	Tinga Layo; 1956; 8p	SATB	$a - g^2$	$G - e^1$	M	Piano	BH	5011
	Wade in the Water; 1941; 7p	SATB/Sop.	$b^b - f^2$ (ab2)	$A^b - f^1$	M	A Cap	Marks	830
	Wade in the Water; 1941; 7p	SSA	$a(f) - a^{b2}$		M	A Cap	Marks	330
CLARY, Salone	The Blind Man Stood on the Road and Cried; 1970; 8p	SATB	$g - f^2$	$F - c^1$	E	A Cap	Warner	WB118
	I Want to Live with God; 1957; 8p	SATB	$g - g^2$	$F - g^1$	E	A Cap	Warner	R3490
	When You Hear Those Bells; 1970; 4p	SATB/Sop.	$b - g^2$	$G - g^1$	E	A Cap	Warner	WB117
	Where Shall I Go?; 1969; 5p	SATB	$b^b - a^{b2}$	$F - b1$	E	A Cap	Warner	W7-1030
COLEMAN, Charles D.	Alleluia; 1976; 13p	SATB	$b^b - g^2$	$F(E^b) - a^1$	M	A Cap	NSMP	1-111
	Blest Be the Tie; 1977; 9p	SATB	$g - a^2$	$E^b - g^1$	M	A Cap	NSMP	1-113
	The Lord's Prayer; 1964; 4p	SATB	$g - f^2$	$F - f^1$	M	A Cap	NSMP	1-110
	O Perfect Love; 1977; 10p	SATB	$a - a^2$	$G - g^1$	M	Piano	NSMP	1-116
	Seeking for That City; 1977; 5p	SATB	$g - a^2$	$G - f^{\#1}$	E	A Cap	NSMP	1-112
COOPER, William B.	Beatitudes; 1966; 46p	SATB			M	Organ	MS	
	Mass for Choir and Congregation; 1973; 9p	SATB	$a - f^2$	$D - b1$	E	Organ	MS	
	Mass of the Poor; 1976; 12p	SATB	$b - a^2$	$G - e^1$	E	Organ	MS	

Composer or Arranger	Title; Copyright Date; Number of Pages	Voicing, Soloist	Vocal Range Women	Vocal Range Men	Range of Difficulty	A Cappella Accompaniment Instrumentation	Publisher	Catalog Number
COOPER (continued)	Mass of the Poor (Spiritual-Deep River); 1976; 7p	SATB	$a - g^2$	$G - f\#^1$	M	Organ	MS	
	Mass to St. Philip (Festival Mass of Thanksgiving); 1979; 50p	SATB/Sop. Alto/Ten.	$g - a^2$	$E - g^1$	M	Organ	MS	
	On a Drop of Dew; 1972; 5p	SATB			M	A Cap	MS	
	The Port Royal Te Deum; 1962; 68p	SATB			M	Organ	MS	
	Psalm 150 (Jubilee); 1975; 25p	SATB/Sop. Bar.	$a^b - c^3$	$G - g^1$	M	Organ	MS	
	The Psalms and Canticles (Protestant Episcopal Church Set to African American Chants) and The Choral Service; 1969; 15p	SATB			E	Organ/A Cap	MS	
	The Royal Banners Forward Go (Palm Sunday); 1955; 12p	SATB	$b - b^2$	$B^b - f\#^1$	M	Organ	MS	
	Te Deum; 1978; 38p	SATB			M	Organ	MS	
	Two Short Anthems; 1955; 4p 1. Come unto Me 2. Jesu, Joy of Man's Desiring	SATB Unison	$g - d^2$	$B^b - c^1$	E	Organ	MS	
CUNNINGHAM, Arthur	Harlem Suite; 1972;							
	1. A Little Love; 19p	SATB	$c^1 - e^{b2}$	$A^b - f^1$	M	Piano	Presser	312-40965
	2. World Goin' Down; 11p	SATB/Alto Sop.	$g - g^{b2}$	$F - b^1$	E	A Cap	Presser	312-40967
	3. Sunday in de Evenin'; 6p	SA	$f - a^{b2}$		M	Piano	Presser	312-40968
	4. Lenox; 6p	SATB/Nar.	$a - a^2$	$F - e^1$	MD	Piano	Presser	312-40982
	5. Munday Man; 8p	SATB	$f - a^{b2}$	$F - g^1$	M	Piano	Presser	312-40983

Composer or Arranger	Title; Copyright Date; Number of Pages	Voicing, Soloist	Vocal Range Women	Vocal Range Men	Range of Difficulty	A Cappella Accompaniment Instrumentation	Publisher	Catalog Number
CUNNINGHAM (continued)	He Met Her at the Dolphin; 1964; 10p	SATB	$b^b - a^{b2}$	$A - f^{\#1}$	M	A Cap	Remick	R 3457
	Hinkty Woman; 1975; 24p (Harlem Suite)	SATB/Ten.	$b^b - b^{b2}$	$B^b - f^1$	M	Piano	Presser	312-41096
	Honey Brown; 1972; 8p	TTBB/Ten. Bar.		$A^b - b1$	M	A Cap	Presser	312-40969
	Sunday Stone; 1974; 12p	SATB	$g - b2$	$G - a^1$	M	Piano/organ	Presser	312-41053
	Timber; 1972; 5p	SATB	$g - a^2$	$G - f^1$	M	A Cap	Presser	312-40970
	Two Prayers: Lord Look Down; We Gonna Make It; 1972; 8p	SATB	$g - a^2$	$F - g^1$	M	A Cap	Presser	312-40966
CURTIS, Marvin	By an' Bye; n.d.; 3p	SATB	$a - d^2$	$G(D) - f^{\#1}$	E	A Cap	MS	
	Christ Is Born; 1978; 8p	SATB	$b - g^2$	$G - g^1$	E	A Cap	Foster	MF-528
	Fanfare - "Noel"; 1979; 3p	SATB	$g - a^2$		E	Brass choir	MS	
	Gloria; 1978; 8p	SATB	$g - a^2$	$d - a^1$	M	A Cap	Foster	MF-179
	Gloria; n.d.; 45p	SATB			M	Orch.	MS	
	Psalm 96; 1976; 6p	SATB	$b^b - g^2$	$d - g^1$	E	A Cap	MS	
	Sit at d'Lamb's Table; 1979; 8p	SATB	$a - e^2$	$G - e^1$	E	A Cap	Foster	MF-188
	Worship the Lord; 1976; 8p	SATB	$b - g^{\#2}$	$A - g^1$	E	A Cap	Foster	MF-168
DA COSTA, Noel George	Ceremony of Spirituals; n.d.; 23p	SATB Double Chorus Solo Quintet	$g - b^{b2}$	$F - b^{b1}$	D	Orch./saxophone	MS	
	Counterpoint; n.d.; 20p		$b^b - c^3$	$A - a^1$	D	Organ	MS	

Composer or Arranger	Title; Copyright Date; Number of Pages	Voicing, Soloist	Vocal Range		Range of Difficulty	A Cappella Accompaniment Instrumentation	Publisher	Catalog Number
			Women	Men				
DA COSTA (continued)	"Five/Seven"; 1969; 3p	SSA	$e^1 - c^2$		MD	Organ/or any 2 instruments	MS	
	I Have a Dream; 1978; 4p	SATB	$a - e^{b2}$	$F - d^{b1}$	M	Organ	Hinshaw	
	I'm So Glad Trouble Don't Last Always; 1962; 8p	SATB/Alto	$a - f^{\#2}$	$F^\# - f^{\#1}$	MD	A Cap	MS	
	Let Down the Bars, O Death; n. d. ; 3p	SATBB	$g - c^2$	$G - f^{\#1}$	MD	A Cap	MS	
	Little Lamb; n. d. ; 4p	SATB	$b - b^2$	$F - a^1$	MD	A Cap	MS	
	O God of Light and Love; n. d. ; 4p	Unison	$c^1 - d^2 (e^{b2})$	$c - d^1 (e^{b1})$	M	Organ	MS	
	Through the Valley; n. d. ; 3p	SATB	$f^\# - g^2$	$c - f^{\#1}$	MD	A Cap	MS	
	Two Shaker Songs: Our Heavenly Father, Again O Heavenly Father; 1964; 7p	SATB	$b - f^2$	$F - b^1$	M	A Cap	MS	
	We Are Climbing Jacob's Ladder; n. d. ; 6p	SATB	$g - b^2$	$G - g^1$	M	A Cap	MS	
DAVIS, Elmer	Chillun!; 1957; 7p	SATB/Ten. Bar.	$b^b - g^2 (c^3)$	$F - g^1$	M	A Cap	CF	CM-6948
	Mary's Little Baby; 1963; 8p	SATB/Sop. Ten.	$a - e^2$	$F(E) - e^1$	M	A Cap	GS	11076
	You Gotta Cross the River When You Die; 1958; 11p	SATB	$b^b - a^2$	$F - e^{b1}$	MD	A Cap	GS	10601
DAWSON, William L.	Ain'a That Good News; 1937; 8p	SATB	$a - a^2$	$F - f^1$	MD	A Cap	Kjos	T103
	Ain'a That Good News; 1937; 8p	TTBB		$F - a^1$	MD	A Cap	Kjos	T104

Composer or Arranger	Title; Copyright Date; Number of Pages	Voicing, Soloist	Vocal Range		Range of Difficulty	A Cappella Accompaniment Instrumentation	Publisher	Catalog Number
			Women	Men				
DAWSON (continued)	Before the Sun Goes Down (arr. of Londonderry Air); 1978; 10p	SATB	$g - b^2$	$E - g^1$	M	Piano	Kjos	ED 5951
	Behold the Star; 1946; 10p	SATB/Sop. Ten.	$c^1 - a^2$	$F - f^1$	M	A Cap	Kjos	T111
	Every Time I Feel the Spirit; 1946; 8p	SATB	$b^b - g^2$	$G - b^1$ (E^b)	M	A Cap	Kjos	T117
	Every Time I Feel the Spirit; 1946; 8p	TTBB/Bar.		$E - b^1$	M	A Cap	Kjos	T125
	Every Time I Feel the Spirit; 1946; 8p	SSAA	$g^\# - a^2$		M	A Cap	Kjos	T126
	Ezekiel Saw de Wheel; 1942; 15p	SATB	$b^b - b^2$	$G - g^1$	MD	A Cap	Kjos	T110
	Feed-A My Sheep; 1971; 11p	TTBB		$D - a^1$	MD	Piano	Kjos	T133
	Feed-A My Sheep; 1971; 11p	SATB	$g - a^2$	$F - f^1$	MD	Piano	Kjos	T134
	Feed-A My Sheep; 1971; 11p	SSAA	$g - a^2$		MD	Piano	Kjos	T135
	Hail Mary; 1949; 12p	SATB	$a - g^2$	$G - f^1$	MD	A Cap	Kjos	T112
	Hail Mary; 1946; 12p	TTBB		$G - g^1$	MD	A Cap	Kjos	T113
	I Wan' to Be Ready; 1967; 15p	SATB/Alto Bar.	$a - g^{\#2}$	$F - g^1$	MD	A Cap	Kjos	T127
	I Wan' to Be Ready; 1967; 15p	TTBB/Ten.		$E - g^{\#1}$	MD	A Cap	Kjos	T123
	I Wan' to Be Ready; 1967; 15p	SSAA	$g - g^{\#2}$		MD	A Cap	Kjos	T129
	In His Care-O; 1961; 14p	SATB	$b^b - a^2$	$B^b - f^1$	MD	A Cap	Kjos	T122
	In His Care-O; 1961; 14p	TTBB		$F - a^1$	MD	A Cap	Kjos	T123
	Jesus Walked This Lonesome Valley; 1927; 6p	SATB	$g - g^2$	$G - g^1$	M	Piano	Warner	GS21

Composer or Arranger	Title; Copyright Date; Number of Pages	Voicing, Soloist	Vocal Range – Women	Vocal Range – Men	Range of Difficulty	A Cappella Accompaniment Instrumentation	Publisher	Catalog Number
DAWSON (continued)	Jesus Walked This Lonesome Valley; 1927; 11p	TTBB/Bar.		$G - a^1$	M	Piano	Warner	C10783
	King Jesus Is A-Listening; 1925; 6p	SATB	$b^b - b^2$	$A^b - f^1$	M	A Cap	FS	2004
	Lit'l' Boy Chile; 1942; 9p	SATB/Sop. Bass; Bar.	$b^b - f^2$	$F - g^1$	M	A Cap	Kjos	T120
	Mary Had a Baby; 1947; 9p	SATB/Sop.	$g - g^2$	$G - g^1$	MD	A Cap	Kjos	T118
	Mary Had a Baby; 1947; 6p	TTBB/Ten.		$G - g^1$	M	A Cap	Kjos	T119
	My Lord What a Mourning; 1954; 4p	SATB	$g^\# - g^{\#2}$	$E - f^{\#1}$	MD	A Cap	FS	2009
	Oh, What a Beautiful City; 1934; 11p	SATB	$c^1 - a^2$	$F - g^1$	D	A Cap	Kjos	T100
	Out in the Fields; 1929; 10p	SATB	$b^b - b^2$	$G - g^1$	M	Piano	Kjos	T130
	Out in the Fields; 1929; 8p	SSA	$g - a^{b2}$		M	Piano	Kjos	T131
	The Rugged Yank; 1920; 15p	TTBB		$F - a^1$	M	Piano	Kjos	T132
	Slumber Song; 1964; 11p	SSA	$g - g^{\#2}$		M	Piano	Kjos	T137
	Slumber Song; 1964; 11p	SATB	$g^\# - g^{\#2}$	$F - e^1$	M	Piano	Kjos	T138
	Soon Ah Will Be Done; 1934; 11p	TTBB		$G - g^1$	MD	A Cap	Kjos	T101A
	Soon Ah Will Be Done; 1947; 11p	SATB	$b - f^{\#2}$	$B - f^{\#1}$	MD	A Cap	Kjos	T102A
	Steal Away; 1942; 10p	SATB	$a - g^2$	$F - f^1$	M	A Cap	Kjos	T108
	Steal Away; 1942; 10p	TTBB/Ten.		$F - a^1$	M	A Cap	Kjos	T109
	Swing Low, Sweet Chariot; 1949; 5p	SATB/Sop.	$c^1 - f^2$	$A^b - b^1$	M	A Cap	Kjos	T114
	Swing Low, Sweet Chariot; 1946; 5p	TTBB		$F - a^{b1}$	M	A Cap	Kjos	T115
	Swing Low, Sweet Chariot; 1949; 5p	SSA/Sop.	$g - e^2$		M	A Cap	Kjos	T116

Composer or Arranger	Title; Copyright Date; Number of Pages	Voicing, Soloist	Vocal Range (Women)	Vocal Range (Men)	Range of Difficulty	A Cappella Accompaniment Instrumentation	Publisher	Catalog Number
DAWSON (continued)	Talk About a Child That Do Love Jesus; 1927; 6p	SATB	g – g^2	G – g^1	MD	Piano	Kjos	2015
	There Is a Balm in Gilead; 1939; 8p	SATB/Sop.	a – d^2	D – $f^{\#1}$	M	A Cap	Kjos	T105
	There Is a Balm in Gilead; 1939; 8p	TTBB/Ten.		E^b – g^1	M	A Cap	Kjos	T106
	There Is a Balm in Gilead; 1939; 8p	SSA/Sop.	g – e^{b2}		M	A Cap	Kjos	T107
	There's a Lit'l Wheel A-Turning; 1949; 12p	SATB	g – f^2	F – f^1	MD	A Cap	Kjos	T121
	Zion's Walls; 1961; 16p	SATB/Sop.	g – g^2	F – g^1	MD	A Cap	Kjos	T124
DE PAUR, Leonard	Alexander (Nigerian Work Song); 1964; 5p	TTBB		E – $f^{\#1}$	E	Drums	LC	
	All 'Round de Glory Manger; 1958; 11p	TTBB		F – b^1	MD	A Cap	LG	709
	Ay, Ay, Ay; 1957; 12p	SATB/Ten.	b^b – g^2	E^b – g^1	MD	A Cap	LG	654
	Eh Onchiri Oyo; 1964; 5p	Male Chorus/Leader		c – a^1	E	Bottles/drum	LC	
	Git on Down Dat Road; 1963; 5p	TTBB		A^b – b^1	M	A Cap	LC	
	God Rest Ye Merry, Gentlemen; 1956; 7p	TTBB/Ten.		$F^\#$ – b^1	M	A Cap	LG	545
	Good Evening, Mrs. Flanagan; 1960; 16p	SATB/Bar. Alto	e^1 – a^2	F – a^1	M	A Cap	LG	886
	In Bright Mansions Above; 1960; 7p	SATB	$g^\#$ – b^2	$G^\#$ – $g^{\#1}$	M	A Cap	LG	926
	Jerry; 1954; 15p	TTBB		$D^\#$ – a^1	M	A Cap	LG	522
	Jesus Hung and Died; 1960; 24p	SATB/Bar. Ten.; Sop.	d^1 – b^{b2}	G – g^1	M	A Cap	LG	829

Composer or Arranger	Title; Copyright Date; Number of Pages	Voicing, Soloist	Vocal Range		Range of Difficulty	A Cappella Accompaniment Instrumentation	Publisher	Catalog Number
			Women	Men				
DE PAUR (continued)	Kro Kro, Hinh Hinh!; 1964; 5p	TTBB/Solo		$A - a^1$	E	Castanet/drum	LC	
	Kufidimpala Bituta; 1963; 7p	SSA/Sop.	$b^b - d^2$		E	A Cap	LC	
	Kwagyansa, Menna Bio; 1964; 3p	Male Chorus/Solo		$d - c^1$	E	Castanet, gong, medium drum, large drum	LC	
	Marry a Woman Uglier Than You; 1954; 12p	TTBB		$E - b^1$	MD	A Cap	LG	543
	Nobody Knows de Trouble I See; 1954; 10p	TTBB		$E - g\#^1$	M	A Cap	LG	524
	Oh Po' Little Jesus; 1958; 6p	TTBB		$F - a^1$	MD	A Cap	LG	710
	Pauline, Pauline; 1969; 11p	TTBB		$F - a^1$	M	A Cap	LG	51466
	Swing Low, Sweet Chariot; 1954; 7p	TTBB		$D - g^1$	E	A Cap	LG	523
	Ye Ke Omo Mi; 1965; 9p	SATB	$c^1 - c^3$	$c - a^1$	M	A Cap	LG	51213
	Ye Ke Omo Mi; 1965; 10p	TTBB		$B^b - b^1$	M	A Cap	LG	51213
DETT, R. Nathaniel	As by the Streams of Babylon; 1933; 4p	SATB/Sop.	$a - f^2$	$G - d^1$	E	A Cap	GS	7713
	Ask for the Old Poets; 1941; 12p	SATB	$g - a^2$	$F - g^1$	M	A Cap	Mills	
	Ave Maria; 1978; 7p	SATB	$g - a^2$	$F - g^1$	M	A Cap	Hinshaw	HMC 333
	The Chariot Jubilee; 1919; 31p	SATB	$a - a^2$	$G - g^1$	M	Organ	JC	35221
	City of God; 1941; 12p	SATB	$g - a^2$	$A - g^1$	M	Piano/organ	JF	7736
	The Dett Collection of Spirituals (originals, settings, anthems, motets); 1936 [See "Collections of Spirituals"]	SATB				A Cap & Piano	HM	HM Auditorium Series #13
	Group I							

Composer or Arranger	Title; Copyright Date; Number of Pages	Voicing, Soloist	Vocal Range — Women	Vocal Range — Men	Range of Difficulty	A Cappella Accompaniment Instrumentation	Publisher	Catalog Number
	Group II Group III Group IV							#14 #15 #16
DETT (continued)	Done Paid My Vow to the Lord; 1919; 8p	SSA/Bar. Alto	$g - g^2$		E	Piano	Presser	322-35007
	Don't Be Weary, Traveler; 1921; 16p	SATB	$a - a^2$	$F^\# - g^1$	M	A Cap	JC	35021
	Don't You Weep No More, Mary; 1930; 8p	SATB	$a - a^2$	$f(D) - f^1$	M	A Cap	GS	7395
	Drink to Me Only with Thine Eyes; 1933; 12p	SATB	$g - g^2$	$G - g^1$	M	A Cap	JF	6700
	Gently, Lord, O Gently Lead Us; 1914; 16p	SATB	$g - g^2$	$F - g^1$	M	A Cap	JC	35164
	Go Not Far from Me, O God; 1933; 11p	SATB	$g - a^2$	$F - a^1$	M	A Cap	JF	6698
	Heavenly Union; 1941; 13p	SATB	$g - a^2$	$F - f^1$	M	A Cap	Mills	4435
	I'll Never Turn Back No More; 1918; 8p	SATB/Sop.	$a - a^2$	$F - f^1$	M	A Cap	JF	
	I'm So Glad Trouble Don't Last Alway; 1919; 4p	SSA	$f - f^2$		M	A Cap	Presser	322-35123
	Juba (From the Suite "In the Bottoms"; text by Dett); 1934; 17p	SATB	$g - a^2$	$F - a^1$	MD	Piano	Clayton F. Summy	
	The Lamb; 1938; 7p	SSA	$e^\# - g^{\#2}$		E	A Cap	JF	7401
	Let Us Cheer the Weary Traveler; 1926; 11p	SATB	$g - e^2$	$G - f^1$	M	A Cap	JF	322-35044
	Listen to the Lambs; 1914; 11p	SATB	$a - a^2$	$F - g^1$	MD	A Cap	GS	8010
	Music in the Mine; 1916; 16p	SATB	$b^b - a^{b2}$	$F - a^{b1}$	M	A Cap	GS	6580

Composer or Arranger	Title, Copyright Date; Number of Pages	Voicing, Soloist	Vocal Range Women	Vocal Range Men	Range of Difficulty	A Cappella Accompaniment Instrumentation	Publisher	Catalog Number
DETT (continued)	Now Rest Beneath Night's Shadow; 1938; 8p	SSAA	$e^b - a^2$		M	A Cap	JF	7399
	O Holy Lord; 1916; 8p	SATB	$g - g^2$	$E - e^1$	M	A Cap	GS	6579
	The Ordering of Moses (Oratorio); 1939; 123p	SATB/Sop. Alto; Ten. Bar.			MD	Full orch.	JF	7230
	Rise Up Shepherd and Follow; 1936; 7p	SATB/Sop. Ten.	$g - d^{b2}$	$E^b - d^{b1}$	E	Piano	JF	7218
	Rise Up Shepherd and Follow; 1936; 7p	TTBB		$G - f^1$	E	Piano	JF	7219
	Sit Down, Servant, Sit Down; 1932; 11p	SATB	$c^1 - g^2$	$G - g^1$	M	Piano	GS	7931
	So, We'll Go No More A-Roving; 1940; 8p	SSAA	$d - c^3$		M	A Cap	JF	7656
	Somebody's Knocking at Your Door; 1921; 16p	SSA	$f^\# - g^2$		M	Piano	JC	35186
	Somebody's Knocking at Your Door; 1939; 16p	SATB	$g - a^2$	$D - g^1$	M	Piano	JC	35197
	Son of Mary; 1926; 15p	SATB	$a - f^{\#2}$	$G^\# - f^{\#1}$	M	A Cap	JC	322-35390
	There's a Meeting Here Tonight; 1921; 11p	SSA	$g - g^2$		M	Piano	JC	35008
	Wasn't That a Mighty Day?; 1933; 11p	SATB/Alto Bar.	$a - a^2$	$F - f^1$	M	A Cap	GS	7712
	Weeping Mary; 1918; 8p	SATB/Sop.	$g - a^2$	$F - a^1$	M	A Cap	JF	4434

Composer or Arranger	Title; Copyright Date; Number of Pages	Voicing, Soloist	Vocal Range Women	Vocal Range Men	Range of Difficulty	A Cappella Accompaniment Instrumentation	Publisher	Catalog Number
DETT (continued)	When I Survey the Wondrous Cross; 1941; 12p	SSAA	e – a²		M	A Cap	Mills	
DUNCAN, John	Burial of Moses (Cantata); 1972; 114p	SATB/Alto		A – g¹	MD	Wind Symphony	MS	
FAX, Mark	You're Tired Chile; 1972; 11p	SATB/Ten.	a – a²	A♭ – c¹	E	Piano	Standard	C617-MXI
	As the Hart Panteth; 1951; 2p	SAB	b – f²	G – g¹	M	A Cap	MS	
	As the Hart Panteth; n. d.; 10p	SATB	g – g²	G – f#¹	M	A Cap	MS	
	Choric Song; n. d.; 6p	SATB	a – g²	G – f#¹	M	A Cap	MS	
	Christ Is Risen; n. d.; 1p	SAB	a – f²	c – d¹	E	A Cap	MS	
	Done Crossed Every Mountain (from the opera "Til Victory Is Won"); 1967; 15p	SATB	b – a²	G – f#¹	MD	Piano/orch.	MS	
	Ev'ry Time I Feel the Spirit; n. d.; 1p	SATB/Alto	b – d²	A – d¹	E	A Cap	MS	
	Except the Lord Build This House; 1957; 7p	SATB	b – g#²	F# – g¹	M	Organ	MS	
	Four Spirituals: Choir No. 2 Series; 1952; 4p	SATB	f# – b2	A♭ – f¹	E	A Cap	MS	
	The Gettysburg Address; 1966; 20p	SATB/Sop. Ten.	g – a♭2	F# – g¹	MD	Piano/orch.	MS	
	Go Tell It on the Mountain; 1939; 7p	SATB/Bass	d¹ – f²	G – f¹	M	A Cap	Presser	21393
	Hail the Crown: Old Negro Melody; 1969; 1p	SATB	b – e²	G – g¹	E	A Cap	MS	
	Hallelujah; 1971; 11p	SATB	a – g²	F# – g¹	MD	A Cap	MS	

Composer or Arranger	Title; Copyright Date; Number of Pages	Voicing, Soloist	Vocal Range Women	Vocal Range Men	Range of Difficulty	A Cappella Accompaniment Instrumentation	Publisher	Catalog Number
FAX (continued)	The Harp of the Wind; 1948; 7p	SATB	b - f#2	A - e1	M	Piano	MS	
	He Hath Shown Thee, O Man; 1974; 3p	SATB	a - g2	G - g1	MD	A Cap	MS	
	Home in That Rock; n.d.; 3p	SSA	f - f2		M	A Cap	MS	
	Hope Thou in God; 1961; 5p	SATB	b - f#2	A - g1	M	Organ	MS	
	I Have a Dream; 1971; 4p	SATB	g - g2	B - f#1	M	A Cap	MS	
	In My Father's House Are Many Mansions; 1968; 2p	SATB	bb - f2	Bb - f1	M	A Cap	MS	
	The Lord Is My Light; 1950; 6p	SAB	b - g2	c - d1	M	Organ/piano	MS	
	Make a Joyful Noise; n.d.; 6p	SATB	c1 - g2	A - f1	M	Organ	MS	
	Old Southern Melody for Voice and Instruments; n.d.; 6p	SATB	c1 - e2	F# - e1	M	Flute, bells, snare drum, harp	MS	
	Out of the Depths; n.d.; 6p	SATB	a - a2	G - f#1	M	A Cap	MS	
	Poem of America (Whitman); 1957; 38p	SATB/Bar.	g - a2	G# - f1	MD	Piano	MS	
	Praise Ye the Lord; 1949; 2p	SAB	b - a2	B - f1	M	A Cap	MS	
	Psalm 67; n.d.; 6p	SATB	a - g2	A - f#1	M	Piano	MS	
	Psalm 121; n.d.; 2p	SAB/Sop.	c1 - g2	Bb - d1	E	A Cap	MS	
	Remember Now Thy Creator; 1949; 11p	SATB	g - a2	E - g1	MD	A Cap	MS	
	Rhapsody on Psalm 127; n.d.; 38p	SATB	b - a2	A - f#1	MD	Orch.	MS	
	Rise Up Shepherd and Follow; 1963; 1p	SATB	ab - eb2	Ab - eb1	E	A Cap	MS	
	'Round the Glory Manger; 1943; 1p	SATB	d1 - g2	G - e1	E	A Cap	MS	

Composer or Arranger	Title; Copyright Date; Number of Pages	Voicing, Soloist	Vocal Range		Range of Difficulty	A Cappella Accompaniment Instrumentation	Publisher	Catalog Number
			Women	Men				
FAX (continued)	Serenade; 1952; 5p	TTBB		$E - g^1$	MD	A Cap	MS	
	A Shining Light (from the opera "Til Victory Is Won"); 1967; 8p	SATB	$c^1 - g^2$	$A - g^1$	D	Piano/orch.	MS	
	Six Folk Anthems; 1938; 19p	SATB	$g - g^2$	$G - g^1$	E	A Cap	MS	
	1. Jacob's Ladder							
	2. O By and By							
	3. My Way Is Cloudy							
	4. Wade in the Water							
	5. Go Tell It on the Mountain (out)							
	6. Walk with Me							
	Song of Praise; 1948; 7p	SATB	$b - f^2$	$G^\# - f^1$	M	Piano	MS	
	Sonnet; 1952; 6p	TTBB		$F - a^1$	MD	A Cap	MS	
	Steal Away to Jesus; n. d. ; 1p	SATB	$a - d^2$	$G - e^1$	E	Organ/piano	MS	
	Study War No More, n. d. ; 1p	SATB	$c^1 - d^{b2}$	$A^b - e^1$	E	A Cap	MS	
	This Little Light of Mine; 1969; 1p	SATB	$a - f^2$	$F - f^1$	E	A Cap	MS	
	We Shall Overcome; 1964; 1p	SATB	$b - f^{\#2}$	$G^\# - f^{\#1}$	E	A Cap	MS	
	Were You There?; 1968; 4p	TTBB		$G - g^1$	E	A Cap	MS	
	Whatsoever a Man Soweth; 1958; 7p	SATB	$c^{\#1} - f^{\#2}$	$G - f^{\#1}$	E	Organ	Augsburg	1229
	Who Can Find a Virtuous Woman; 1953; 3p	SATB	$d^1 - g^2$	$B^b - e^1$	M	A Cap	MS	
FURMAN, James	Ave Maria; 1971; 3p	SATB	$b - f^2$	$F - e^1$	M	A Cap	MS	
	Bye, Bye, Lully, Lullay; 1980; 2p	SATB/Mez.	$a - e^2$	$A - e^1$	M	A Cap	MS	
	Come Thou Long Expected Jesus; 1980; 7p	SATB	$g - e^2$	$F - f^1$	MD	A Cap	Music 70	M70-298

Composer or Arranger	Title; Copyright Date; Number of Pages	Voicing, Soloist	Vocal Range		Range of Difficulty	A Cappella Accompaniment Instrumentation	Publisher	Catalog Number
			Women	Men				
FURMAN (continued)	Four Little Foxes; 1971; 11p 1. Speak Gently 2. Walk Softly 3. Go Lightly 4. Step Softly	SATB	$g - g^2$	$E - g^{\#1}$	MD	A Cap	Oxford	95-309
	Hehlehlooyuh: A Joyful Expression; 1978; 8p	SATB	$b^b - a^2(c^3)$	$G - f^{\#1}$	MD	A Cap	Hinshaw	HMC-312
	Hold On; 1981; 11p	SATB	$c^1 - g^2$	$d - g^1$	MD	Piano/electric organ	Music 70	M70-326
	I Have a Dream (Oratorio); 1970; 57p	SATB Gospel Chorus; Bar. Solo			D	Rock combo	MS	
	Jupiter Shall Emerge; 1978; 17p	SATB	$b - a^2$	$E - a^1$	D	A Cap	MS	
	The Quiet Life; 1968; 20p	SATB	$b^b - a^2$	$F - g^1$	M	A Cap	MS	
	1. Fanfare and Pastorale; 1968 2. Quiet by Day; 1980 3. Sound Sleep by Night; 1980 4. Thus Let Me Live; 1968						MS Music 70 Music 70 MS	M70-293 M70-293
	Rejoice, Give Thanks and Sing; 1980; 5p	SATB	$g - f^2$	$G - g^1$	E	Organ/piano	MS	
	Salve Regina; 1966; 3p	SSATB	$a - g^{\#2}$	$F - e^1$	MD	A Cap	MS	
	Three Responses for Church Service; 1980; 2p	SATB	$a - g^2$	$G - g^1$	E	Organ	MS	
GILLUM, Ruth Helen	Choric Dance; 1951; 8p	SATB	$d^1 - b^2$	$G - d^1$	E	A Cap	JF	8599
	Roll Jordan Roll; 1947; 8p	SATB	$d^{b1} - b^2$	$E^b - g^1$	M	A Cap	JF	8390

Composer or Arranger	Title; Copyright Date; Number of Pages	Voicing, Soloist	Vocal Range Women	Vocal Range Men	Range of Difficulty	A Cappella Accompaniment Instrumentation	Publisher	Catalog Number
GILLUM (continued)	There's No Hiding Place; 1948; 4p	SATB	$b1 - c^2$	$A^b - f^1$	E	A Cap	JF	8756
GREGORY, Percy	Lift Ev'ry Voice; n.d.; 9p	SATB	$d^1 - b^2$	$c - g^{\#1}$	MD	A Cap	MS	
	The Lord Tryeth the Heart; 1978; 7p	SATB	$c^1 - b^{b2}$	$c - g^1$	MD	Piano	MS	
HAILSTORK, Adolphus, III	The Battle; 1968; 3p	TTBB		$E - A^b$	M	A Cap	MS	
	A Carol for All Children; n.d.; 1p	SATB	$b^b - c^2$	$F - e^{b1}$	E	A Cap	MS	
	Cease Sorrows Now; 1979; 7p	SATB	$g^\# - f^2$	$G - f^1$	M	A Cap	Marks	MC4680
	The Cloths of Heaven; 1979; 5p	SATB	$g^\# - f^2$	$F - f^1$	M	A Cap	MS	
	In Memoriam (Langston Hughes); 1967; 4p	SATB	$g^\# - g^2$	$F^\# - g^1$	M	A Cap	MS	
	Mourn Not the Dead; 1969; 9p	SATB	$a - a^{b2}$	$F - g^1$	MD	A Cap	MS	
	My Name Is Toil; 1972; 10p	SATB	$b^b - a^2$	$G - g^1$	M	Brass & Percussion	MS	
	Serenade; 1971; 15p	SSA/Sop.	$c^1 - a^2$		M	Piano/violin	MS	
	Set Me as a Seal upon Thine Heart; 1979; 7p	SATB	$a^\# - a^{b2}$	$E - g^1$	MD	A Cap	MS	
	The Silver Swan; 1968; 3p	SATB	$g - e^2$	$A - g^1$	M	A Cap	MS	
HAIRSTON, Jacqueline	Nowhere to Lay His Head; 1971; 6p	SATB	$b - g^2$	$G - e^1$	E	A Cap	Marks	4556
HAIRSTON, Jester	Amen; 1957; 7p	SSA/Alto	$a - g^{\#2}$		M	A Cap	Sch	B200394-353

Composer or Arranger	Title; Copyright Date; Number of Pages	Voicing, Soloist	Vocal Range — Women	Vocal Range — Men	Range of Difficulty	A Cappella Accompaniment Instrumentation	Publisher	Catalog Number
HAIRSTON (continued)	Amen; 1957; 10p	SAB/Sop.	a – f#2	c – b1	E	Piano	Bourne	B200394-356
	Amen; 1957; 6p	SATB/Sop. Ten.	b – g2	G – f1	M	A Cap	Bourne	B200394-357
	Amen; 1957; 7p	TTBB/Ten.		G – g1	M	A Cap	Sch	B200394-355
	Angels Rolled de Stone Away; 1949; 7p	SATB	c1 – b2	F – f1	M	Piano	Bourne	B200543-358
	Band of Angels; 1940; 8p	SATB	b1 – a2	Ab – f1	MD	A Cap	Warner	W3671
	Christmas Gift; 1955; 16p	SATB	d1 – f2 (ab2)	G – b1	M	Piano	Bourne	B202325-358
	Christmas Gift; 1955; 16p	SSAB	bb – a2	c – e1	M	Piano	Bourne	B202325-357
	Christmas in de Tropics; 1970; 9p	SATB/Ten.	d1 – e2	Bb – e1	M	A Cap	Bourne	B214466-357
	Crucifixion; 1952; 5p	SATB	f# – f#2	F – g1	M	A Cap	Bourne	B202861-357
	Deep River; 1951; 5p	SATB/Alto	b – f#2	F# – g#1	M	A Cap	Sch	B203182-357
	'Dis Ol' Hammer; 1957; 9p	SATB	b – g2	G – e1	M	A Cap	Bourne	B203257-357
	'Dis Train; 1954; 11p	SATB	b – g2	G – d1	MD	A Cap	Bourne	B203265-357
	Don't Be Weary, Traveler; 1955; 5p	SATB	g – a2	G – e1	E	A Cap	Bourne	B203489-357
	Elijah Rock; 1956; 10p	SSA	f – g2		M	A Cap	Bourne	B203737-353

Composer or Arranger	Title; Copyright Date; Number of Pages	Voicing, Soloist	Vocal Range		Range of Difficulty	A Cappella Accompaniment Instrumentation	Publisher	Catalog Number
			Women	Men				
HAIRSTON (continued)	Elijah Rock; 1955; 11p	SATB/Sop.	$g - g^2$	$F - f^1$	MD	A Cap	Bourne	B203737-358
	Faith Unlocks the Door; 1977; 8p	SATB/Sop. Bar.	$a - f^2$	$F - f^1$	E	Piano	HL	08600550
	Free at Last; 1960; 5p	SATB	$b - a^2(b^2)$	$G - e^1$	E	A Cap	Bourne	B230680-358
	Go Down in de Lonesome Valley; 1965; 8p	SATB	$g - a2$	$F - f^1$	M	A Cap	Bourne	B203701-358
	Go Tell It on the Mountain; 1967; 8p	SATB	$d^1 - a^2$	$G - e^1$	E	A Cap	Bourne	B204735-357
	God's Goin' Buil' Up Zion's Wall; 1960; 8p	SATB	$c^1 - b2$	$F - g^1$	M	A Cap	Bourne	B204784-358
	Goin' Down dat Lonesome Road; 1965; 12p	SATB	$g - b2$	$F - f^1$	M	A Cap	Bourne	J-9
	Goodbye Song; 1967; 8p	SATB	$b^b - e^{b2}$	$B^b - b1$	E	Piano	Bourne	B204909-357
	Gossip, Gossip; 1959; 12p	SATB	$c^1 - d^2$	$F - e^1$	E	Piano	Bourne	B204925-357
	Great God A'Mighty; 1959; 8p	SATB	$c^1 - b2$	$G - g^1$	MD	A Cap	Bourne	B205047-358
	Hand Me Down; 1961; 7p	SATB	$b - g^2$	$G - e^1$	E	A Cap	Bourne	B205260-357
	He's Gone Away; 1957; 7p	SSA	$a - e^2$		E	A Cap	Bourne	B205534-353
	Hold My Mule While I Dance, Josey; 1960; 9p	SATB	$b^b - b2$	$B^b - E^{b1}$	E	Piano	Bourne	B205583-357

Composer or Arranger	Title; Copyright Date; Number of Pages	Voicing, Soloist	Vocal Range		Range of Difficulty	A Cappella Accompaniment Instrumentation	Publisher	Catalog Number
			Women	Men				
HAIRSTON (continued)	Hold On; 1955; 9p	SATB	$a^b - a^2$	$F - f^1$	MD	A Cap	Bourne	B205591-357
	Home in Dat Rock; 1957; 14p	SATB	$b - f^2$	$F - g^1$	MD	Piano	Bourne	B205674-357
	I Can Tell the World; 1959; 11p	SATB	$c^1 - a^2$	$c - f^1$	MD	A Cap	Bourne	B205656-358
	I Want Jesus; 1958; 9p	SATB	$d^1 - g^2$	$G - f^1$	M	A Cap	Bourne	B206151-357
	I'm a Travelin' Man; 1963; 7p	SATB	$c - a^2$	$A - f^1$	M	Piano	Warner	W3712
	In Dat Great Gittin' Up Mornin'; 1952; 9p	SATB/Ten.	$g - g^2 (b^b)$	$G - b1$	E	A Cap	Bourne	B206516-357
	It's All Over Me; 1952; 9p	SATB/Alto	$c^1 - g^2$	$F(D) - g^1$	M	A Cap	Bourne	B206920-357
	Joshua Fit de Battle of Jericho; 1952; 11p	SATB	$c^1 - b^2$	$E - a^1$	MD	A Cap	Bourne	B207142-357
	Let the Church Roll On; 1951; 2p	SSAA	$a^b - f^2$	$G - e^1$	E	A Cap	Bourne	B207548-353
	Little David, Play on Your Harp; 1976; 8p	SATB	$b - a^{b2}$	$G - e^1$	E	A Cap	HL	08601000
	Live-A Humble; 1955; 7p	SATB	$c^1 - g^2$	$A - f^1$	MD	A Cap	Bourne	B207779-357
	Mary, Mary, Where Is Your Baby?; 1950; 6p	SATB	$b^b - g^2$	$G - d^1$	E	A Cap	Bourne	B208215-357
	Mary's Little Boy Chile; 1956; 11p	SATB/Mez.	$c^1 - f^2$	$A - e^1$	MD	Piano	Bourne	B208223-357
	Mornin'; 1952; 9p	SATB/Ten.	$a - b^2$	$G - g^1$	E	A Cap	Sch	S-1013

Composer or Arranger	Title; Copyright Date; Number of Pages	Voicing, Soloist	Vocal Range		Range of Difficulty	A Cappella Accompaniment Instrumentation	Publisher	Catalog Number
			Women	Men				
HAIRSTON (continued)	No Ne Li Domi (You Can't Dance with Me); 1971; 9p	TTBB		$B^b - f^1$	E	A Cap	Bourne	B209049-355
	Oh, Holy, Lord; 1950; 4p	SATB	$b - e^2$	$E - g^1$	M	A Cap	Bourne	B209601-357
	Oh, Rock-a My Soul; 1950; 7p	SATB	$c^1 - a^2$	$F - f^1$	E	A Cap	Bourne	B209627-357
	Our Troubles Was Hard; 1961; 14p	SATB	$b - g^2$	$B - e^1$	MD	A Cap	Bourne	B209924-358
	Poor Man Lazarus; 1955; 5p	SSA	$b - g^2$		E	A Cap	Bourne	B210393-353
	Poor Man Lazarus; 1950; 8p	SATB	$d^1 - g^2$	$G - g^1$	E	A Cap	Bourne	B210393-358
	Ring de Christmas Bells; 1972; 13p	SATB/Sop.	$d^1 - a^{b2}$	$G - e^1$	M	Piano	Bourne	B216523-357
	Rise Up, Shepherd and Follow; 1974; 5p	SATB	$a - d^2$	$G - e^1$	E	A Cap	Bourne	B224170-358
	Sakura, Sakura; 1959; 6p	SATB	$a - d^2$	$G - e^1$	E	Piano	Bourne	B211276-357
	Sometimes I Feel Like a Motherless Child; 1952; 5p	SATB/Mez.	$f^1 - b^{b2}$	$F - a^{b1}$	E	A Cap	Bourne	B212084-357
	Steal Away; 1951; 5p	SATB	$d^1 - a^2$	$E - f^1$	E	A Cap	Bourne	B212530-357
	Swing a Lady Gum-Pum; 1956; 7p	SATB	$a^b - e^{b2}$	$A^b - e^1$	M	A Cap	Bourne	B212696-357
	Tataleo; 1971; 9p	SATB	$c^1 - c^2$	$c - e^{\#1}$	M	A Cap	Bourne	B212795-357

Composer or Arranger	Title; Copyright Date; Number of Pages	Voicing, Soloist	Vocal Range Women	Vocal Range Men	Range of Difficulty	A Cappella Accompaniment Instrumentation	Publisher	Catalog Number
HAIRSTON (continued)	That Old House Is Ha'nted; 1970; 16p	SATB/Sop. or Ten.	$b^b - g^2$	$G - f^1$	E	Piano	Bourne	B212910-357
	Two Encores; 1968; 5p	SATB	$d - g^2$	$B^b - b1$	E	A Cap	Bourne	B213843-357
	1. Sittin' Round the Fire 2. Uncle Johnny's Mule							
	Wade in de Water; 1950; 7p	SATB	$b - g^2$	$E - e^1$	M	A Cap	Warner	W3670
	We're Goin' to That Ball; 1967; 16p	SATB	$b - g^2$	$F - e^1$	M	Piano	Bourne	B216929-357
	What Kind o' Shoes; 1959; 11p	SATB	$b^b - f^2$	$B^b - e^{b1}$	M	A Cap	Bourne	B214320-357
	Who'll Be a Witness for My Lord; 1959; 11p	SATB	$d^1 - a^2$	$B^b - f^1$	M	A Cap	Bourne	B214650-357
	Wonderful Counselor; 1952; 7p	SATB/Alto	$c^1 - c^3$	$E^b - a^1$	M	A Cap	Bourne	B214908-357
	You Better Mind; 1965; 10p	SATB	$b - b^2$	$G - e^1$	M	A Cap	Bourne	B215129-358
HALL, Frederick Douglass	Deliverance (Oratorio); 1963; 76p	SATB			M	Piano/orch.	Rod	
	Steal Away; 1925; 5p	SATB	$b - e^2$	$G - e^1$	E	A Cap	Rod	1945
	Yonder Come Day; 1955; 6p	SATB/Sop.	$c^1 - a^2$	$A^b - f^1$	M	A Cap	Summy	B-973
HANCOCK, Eugene W.	A Babe Is Born; 1975; 7p	SATB or TTBB	$c^1 - g^2$	$F - e^{b1}$	E	Organ/bells	Mills	CMR3325
	Come Here, Lord; 1973; 11p	SATB	$a - g^2$	$F - g^1$	E	A Cap	JF	FEC10078

Composer or Arranger	Title; Copyright Date; Number of Pages	Voicing, Soloist	Vocal Range Women	Vocal Range Men	Range of Difficulty	A Cappella Accompaniment Instrumentation	Publisher	Catalog Number
HANCOCK (continued)	Introit and Gradual for Easter Day; 1980; 7p	SATB	$a - a^2$	$F - d^1$	E	Organ/wind chimes	MS	
	Lord Jesus Think on Me; 1968; 3p	SATB/Treble Alto; Bar.	$d^{b}1 - f^2$	$f - e^{b}1$	E	Organ	MS	
	Mass (Rite II); 1978; 24p	SATB/Sop. Alto; Bar.	$g^{b} - g^{\#}2$	$G - f^{\#}1$	M	Organ	MS	
	Music for Services for Trial Use; 1972; 32p	Unison/ SATB	$c^1 - g^2$	$c - g^1$	M	Organ	MS	
	O Gracious Light; 1978; 4p	Unison/Solo	$d^1 - d^2$	$d - d^1$	E	Organ	MS	
	O Man Rejoice; 1964; 5p	SATB	$g - a^2$	$G - f^{\#}1$	M	Flutes, vib., Dbl. bass	MS	
	O Taste and See; 1980; 6p	SATB	$b^{b} - f^2$	$G - d^1$	E	Organ	Gray	G-CMR-3431
	A Palm Sunday Anthem; 1971; 7p	SATB	$e^{b}1 - g^2$	$B^{b} - g^1$	M	A Cap	Gray	3125
	A Short Mass (Rite II); 1980; 7p	Unison	$d^1 - d^2$	$d - d^1$	E	Organ	MS	
	A Song of Creation (Benedictus, Omni Opera Domine); n. d.; 5p	SATB & Congregation	$d^{b}1 - f^2$	$A - c^{\#}1$	E	Organ	MS	
	A Song of Praise (Benedictus es Domine); 1979; 6p	2 equal parts or Congregation			E	Organ	MS	
	There's a Star in the East; 1971; 3p	SATB	$g - g^2$	$G - e^{b}1$	M	A Cap	MS	
	Thirteen Spirituals [See "Collections of Spirituals"]	Unison & two parts				Organ & A Cap	Gray	
	This Is God's Place; n. d.; 17p	SATB/Unison Choir	$a - f^{\#}2$	$F^{\#} - e^{\#}1$	M	Organ/brass quartet/drums	MS	
	Three Carols; n. d.; 9p	SATB	$b - e^2$	$F - e^1$	E	Organ	MS	

Composer or Arranger	Title; Copyright Date; Number of Pages	Voicing, Soloist	Vocal Range Women	Vocal Range Men	Range of Difficulty	A Cappella Accompaniment Instrumentation	Publisher	Catalog Number
HANCOCK (continued)	1. How Brightly Beams the Morning Star 2. Immortal Babe 3. Coventry Carol							
HANDY, William C.	The Bridegroom Has Done Come; 1935; 5p	SATB	$c^1 - f^2$	$F - f^1$	M	Piano	Handy	
	Give Me Jesus; 1927; 4p	SATB/Bass	$b^b - g^2$	$A^b - f^1$	E	Piano	Handy	
	I'll Be There in the Morning; 1933; 7p	SATB	$c^1 - e^{b2}$	$F - f^1$	E	Piano	Handy	
	I'm Drinking from a Fountain; 1925; 6p	SATB	$c^1 - f^2$	$F - f^1$	E	Organ	Handy	
	I've Heard of a City Called Heaven; 1928; 7p	SATB	$g - g^2$	$F - f^1$	E	Piano	Handy	
	Let Us Cheer the Weary Traveler; 1927; 7p	SATB	$g - g^2$	$G - g^1$	E	Piano	Handy	
	Opportunity; 1932; 7p	TTBB		$F - a\,b1$	E	Piano	Handy	
	Saint Louis Blues; 1914; 11p	SATB/Alto	$a - f^2$	$F - g^1$	M	Piano	Handy	
	Saint Louis Blues; 1914; 7p	SA or TB	$a - d^2$	$A - d^1$	E	Piano	Handy	
	Saint Louis Blues; 1914; 7p	SSA or TTB	$g - d^2$	$G - d^1$	M	Piano	Handy	
	Second Collection of 37 Spirituals						Handy	
	Shine Like a Mornin' Star; 1942; 7p	SATB	$b - e^2$	$G - e^1$	E	Piano	Handy	
	They That Sow in Tears; 1940; 7p	SATB	$a - g^2$	$G - f^1$	E	Piano	Handy	
	'Tis the Old Ship of Zion; 1935; 4p	SATB/Bar.	$c^1 - f^2$	$E^b - f^1$	E	Piano	Handy	
	We'll Go On and Serve the Lord; 1931; 6p	SATB/Sop.	$a - a^2$	$G - g^1$	M	Piano	Handy	

Composer or Arranger	Title; Copyright Date; Number of Pages	Voicing, Soloist	Vocal Range — Women	Vocal Range — Men	Range of Difficulty	A Cappella Accompaniment Instrumentation	Publisher	Catalog Number
HARRIS, Robert A.	Benedictus; 1969; 5p	SSAA	g – b^2		MD	A Cap	MS	
	A Collect for Peace; 1972; 21p	SATB	a – b^2	$F^\#$ – $g^{\#1}$	MD	A Cap/brass septet	MS	
	Communion Service; 1974; 12p	Unison	c^1 – f^2	c – f^1	MD	Organ	MS	
	For the Beauty of the Earth; 1970; 6p	SATB	$g^\#$ – b^2	F – e^1	M	Organ/piano	MS	
	Glory to God; 1975; 10p	SATB	a – a^2	G – a^1	D	A Cap	Boonin	
	The Hungry Angels; 15p	SATB	b – a^2	A – g^1	M	A Cap	Foster	MF 191
	Kyrie and Gloria; 1964; 12p	SATB	b – a^2	F – g^1	D	A Cap	MS	
	Let Us Break Bread Together; 1969; 8p	SSAA/Sop.	f – a^{b2}		M	A Cap/flute op.	MS	
	May the Grace of Christ Our Saviour; 1975; 4p	SATB	b – a^2	G – $f^{\#1}$	M	A Cap	MS	
	O Come, Let Us Sing unto the Lord; 1969; 12p	SATB	c^1 – a^2	F – g^1	MD	Organ	MS	
	Rejoice, Ye Pure in Heart; 1968; 8p	SATB	b – a^2	G – $f^{\#1}$ (a^1)	MD	A Cap	MS	
	Three Children's Prayers; 1969; 6p	SSA	g – a^2		M	A Cap	MS	
HICKS, L'Roy	I Couldn't Hear Nobody Pray; 1973; 5p	SATB/Sop. Ten.	b^b – a^2	F(D) – f^1	E	A Cap	Hope	SP712
	Ready; 1973; 2p	TTBB		E^b – b1	E	A Cap	Hope	TB203
JAMES, Willis Laurence	Captin, Look A-yonder; 1953; 8p	TTBB/Ten.		D – g^1	M	A Cap	Remick	9-R-3179
	Here's a Pretty Little Baby; 1976; 6p	SATB	d – g^2	G – d^1	E	A Cap	Schmitt	7627

Composer or Arranger	Title; Copyright Date; Number of Pages	Voicing, Soloist	Vocal Range Women	Vocal Range Men	Range of Difficulty	A Cappella Accompaniment Instrumentation	Publisher	Catalog Number
JAMES (continued)	Negro Bell Carol; 1952; 7p	SATB	$g - g^2$	$D - g^1$	M	A Cap	CF	CM6683
	Oh' Po' Little Jesus; 1937; 6p	SATB/Sop.	$g - f^2$	$F - d^1$	E	A Cap	GS	8170
	Reign, King Jesus; 1952; 8p	SATB/Sop.	$b^b - a^2$	$F - f^1$	M	A Cap	Remick	5-R3177
	Roun' de Glory Manger; 1937; 8p	SATB/Sop. Ten.	$b - g^2$	$G - g^1$	M	A Cap	GS	37886
JESSYE, Eva	The Breeze and I (Leucona); 1928; 10p	SATB	$b^b - b2$	$B - b1$	M	Piano	Marks	13414
	By Heck (Henry); 1925; 10p	SATB	$d^1 - f^2$	$G - a b1$	M	Piano	Marks	13415-8
	I Belong to That Band; 1965; 8p	SATB/Sop. Bass	$b^b - g^2$	$G - g^1$	E	Piano	Skidmore	SK2091
	Move! Let Me Shine; 1965; 6p	SATB	$b^b - b2$	$G - f^1$	M	Piano	Skidmore	SK2093
	Rock, Mt. Sinai; 1965; 5p	SATB	$c^1 - f^2$	$F - f^1$	E	Piano	Skidmore	SK2095
	When the Saints Go Marching In; 1966; 8p	SATB	$c^1 - a2$	$B^b - a^b$	M	Piano	Marks	13416-6
	Who Is That Yonder?; 1965; 6p	SATB	$c^{\#1} - f^2$	$A - f^{\#1}$	E	Piano	Skidmore	SK2096
JOHNSON, Hall	Ain't Got Time to Die; 1955; 16p	SATB/Ten.	$b^b - g^2$	$G - g^1$	M	A Cap	GS	10301
	Cert'n'y Lord; 1930; 11p	SATB/Ten. Bass	$c^1 - f^2$	$F - f^1$	M	A Cap	CF	CM6641
	City Called Heaven; 1930; 7p	SATB	$b - f^{\#2}$	$F^{\#} - f^{\#1}$	E	A Cap	Robbins	R-3303
	Crucifixion; 1953; 9p	SATB/Ten.	$g - g^2 (d^3)$	$D - g^1$	M	A Cap	CF	CM 6501
	Crucifixion; 1953; 8p	TTBB		$D - d^2$	MD	A Cap	CF	CM 6757
	Dere's No Hidin' Place Down Dere; 1930; 7p	SATB	$c^{\#1} - b2$	$G - g^1$	M	A Cap	CF	CM6501

Composer or Arranger	Title; Copyright Date; Number of Pages	Voicing, Soloist	Vocal Range		Range of Difficulty	A Cappella Accompaniment Instrumentation	Publisher	Catalog Number
			Women	Men				
JOHNSON (continued)	Elijah Rock; 1956; 15p	SATB	$a^b - b^1$	$F - b^1$	M	A Cap	GS	10354
	Fix Me Jesus; 1955; 7p	SATB/Sop.	$c^1 - f^2$	$F - f^1$	E	A Cap	GS	10278
	Go Down, Moses; 1930; 7p	SATB/Bar.	$d^1 - g^2$	$G - g^1$	M	A Cap	CF	CM6739
	His Name So Sweet; 1935; 2p	SATB	$c^1 - g^2$	$G - b^1$	E	A Cap	CF	CM4580
	His Name So Sweet; 1935; 3p	SSA	$a - b^2$		E	A Cap	CF	CM5213
	His Name So Sweet; 1935; 3p	TTBB		$G - b^1$	E	Piano	CF	CM2183
	Hol' de Light; 1959; 7p	SATB	$f - f^2$	$F - f^1$	M	A Cap	CF	CM7104
	Honor! Honor!; 1935; 7p	SATB/Ten.	$b - f^{\#2}$	$E - f^{\#1}$	E	A Cap	CF	CM4579
	Honor! Honor!; 1935; 6p	TTBB		$G^{\#} - a^1$	E	A Cap	CF	CM21826
	Honor! Honor!; 1935; 6p	SSA	$b - a^2$		M	Piano	CF	CM5212
	I Cannot Stay Here by Myself; 1940; 6p	SATB/Alto	$b - b^2$	$E - a^1$	M	A Cap	CF	CM4724
	I Got a Mule; 1949; 9p	TTBB		$B^b - g^1$	E	A Cap	Robbins	R3444
	I Got Shoes; 1949; 10p	SATB	$c^1 - e^2$	$G - e^1$	M	A Cap	Robbins	R3413
	I'll Never Turn Back No Mo'; 1949; 7p	SATB	$c^1 - f^2$	$G - f^1$	E	A Cap	Robbins	R3452
	I've Been 'Buked; 1946; 7p	SATB	$b^b - f^2$	$F - e^{b1}$	E	A Cap	GS	9650
	Jesus Lay Your Head in de Winder; 1930; 8p	SATB/Ten.	$b^b - g^2$	$G - e^{b1}$	M	A Cap	Robbins	R3301
	Keep a-Inchin' Along; 1957; 10p	TTBB		$E - a^1$	M	A Cap	GS	10485
	Lord, I Want to Be a Christian; 1946; 9p	SATB/Sop.	$d^1 - g^2$	$G - g^1$	M	A Cap	GS	9561
	Lord, I Don't Feel Noways Tired; 1930; 9p	SATB/Ten.	$c^1 - g^2$	$E^b - g^1$	M	A Cap	CF	CM6502

Composer or Arranger	Title; Copyright Date; Number of Pages	Voicing, Soloist	Vocal Range Women	Vocal Range Men	Range of Difficulty	A Cappella Accompaniment Instrumentation	Publisher	Catalog Number
JOHNSON (continued)	Mary Had a Baby; 1955; 7p	SATB	$d^1 - e^2$	$G - e^1$	M	A Cap	GS	10359
	Oh, Freedom; 1957; 10p	SATB	$d^1 - e^2$	$c - g^1$	E	A Cap	GS	10520
	Oh, Holy Lord; 1957; 9p	SATB	$b - e^2$	$E - g^1$	M	A Cap	GS	10449
	Oh Lord, Have Mercy on Me; 1946; 8p	SATB/Sop.	$a - f^2$	$D - g^1$	M	A Cap	GS	9558
	Nobody Knows the Trouble I See; 1949; 9p	SATB/Ten.	$a^b - a^{b2}$	$A^b - a^{b1}$	E	A Cap	Robbins	R3451
	Ride On, Jesus; 1957; 11p	SATB	$c^1 - a^2$	$F - a^1$	M	A Cap	GS	10483
	Ride On, King Jesus; 1951; 11p	SATB	$a - c^3$	$C - a^{b1}$	MD	A Cap	CF	CM6702
	River Chant; 1947; 7p	SATB/Bar.	$c - b^{b2}$	$A^b - a^{b1}$	E	A Cap	CF	CM6208
	Run Li'l Chillun; 1941; 14p	SATB/Ten.	$a - a^2$	$D - f^1$	M	Piano	Robbins	R2164
	Scandalize My Name; 1958; 13p	SATB/Ten.	$e^1 - f^{\#2}$	$A - e^{\#1}$	M	A Cap	GS	10608
	Sometimes I Feel Like a Motherless Child; 1956; 8p	SATB/Alto	$a - a^2$	$D - f^1$	MD	A Cap	Marks	4007
	Steal Away; 1935; 3p	SSA	$b - b^2$		E	Piano	CF	CM5214
	Steal Away; 1935; 2p	SATB	$d^1 - b^2$	$G - e^1$	E	A Cap	CF	CM4581
	Steal Away; 1935; 2p	TTBB		$G - b^1$	E	A Cap	CF	CM2184
	Swing Dat Hammer; 1958; 10p	TTBB		$E - g^1$	M	A Cap	GS	10643
	Take My Mother Home; 1940; 11p	SATB/Bar.		$F - d^1$	M	A Cap	GS	CM6606
	Trampin'; 1956; 8p	SATB/Alto	$a - a^2$	$F - f^1$	MD	A Cap	Marks	4009
	Walk Together, Chillun; 1956; 15p	SATB	$d^1 - b^2$	$G - g^1$	MD	A Cap	Marks	4006
	'Way Over in Beulah Lan'; 1956; 11p	SATB	$g(f) - c^3$	$F - b^{b1}$	MD	A Cap	Marks	4008

Composer or Arranger	Title; Copyright Date; Number of Pages	Voicing, Soloist	Vocal Range — Women	Vocal Range — Men	Range of Difficulty	A Cappella Accompaniment Instrumentation	Publisher	Catalog Number
JOHNSON (continued)	'Way Up in Heaven; 1930; 5p	SATB	$a - g\#^2$	$E - g^1$	E	Piano	Robbins	R3300
	Were You There?; 1954; 11p	SATB/Sop. Ten.	$d^1 - g^2$	$G - g^1$	E	A Cap	GS	10128
	What Kinder Shoes; 1947; 5p	SATB	$d^1 - e^2$	$G - g^1$	M	A Cap	CF	CM6209
	When I Was Sinking Down; 1946; 9p	SATB	$d^1 - f^2$	$B - g^1$	E	A Cap	GS	9559
	Who Built de Ark; 1954; 13p	TTBB		$G - g^1$	M	A Cap	CF	CM7444
JOHNSON, J. Rosamond	All God's Chillun Got Shoes; 1950; 11p	SATB	$c^1 - b^{b2}$	$F - f^1$	MD	Piano	Handy	
	Didn't My Lord Deliver Daniel; 1938; 11p	SATB/Sop.	$d^1 - g^2$	$C - g^1$	M	Piano	Handy	
	Dry Bones; 1938; 7p	SATB	$c^1 - g^2$	$c - f^1$	M	Piano	Handy	
	Go Chain de Lion Down; 1935; 5p	SATB	$a - f^2$	$G - f^1$	M	Piano	Handy	
	Go Down Moses; 1938; 7p	SATB	$a^b - a^{b2}$	$F - a^{b1}$	M	Piano	Handy	
	I Ain't Goin' Study War No More; 1938; 7p	SATB	$d^{b1} - d^{b2}$	$A^b - e^{b1}$	E	Piano	Handy	
	Joshua Fit de Battle o' Jericho; 1935; 11p	SATB	$c^1 - g^2$	$G - g^1$	M	Piano	Handy	
	Lift Ev'ry Voice and Sing; 1921; 4p	SATB	$c^1 - f^2$	$A^b - g^1$	E	Piano	Marks	831
	Lift Ev'ry Voice and Sing; 1921; 6p	SAB	$b^b - f^2 (a^{b2})$	$c - d^{b1}$	E	Piano	Marks	4523
	O Come Let Us Sing; 1934; 6p	SATB	$c^1 - f^2$	$F - f^1$	E	Piano	Handy	
	O, Wasn't That a Wide River; 1935; 5p	SATB	$b - a^2$	$F - f^1$	E	Piano	Handy	
	Same Train; 1935; 4p	SATB	$b^b - e^2$	$A^b - e^{b1}$	M	Piano	Handy	

Composer or Arranger	Title; Copyright Date; Number of Pages	Voicing, Soloist	Vocal Range Women	Vocal Range Men	Range of Difficulty	A Cappella Accompaniment Instrumentation	Publisher	Catalog Number
JOHNSON (continued)	Stan' Still Jordan; 1926; 4p	SATB	$c^{\#1} - a^2$	$G - g^1$		A Cap	Flammer	1025
	Steal Away to Jesus; 1937; 7p	SATB/Alto Bar.		$G - g^1$	MD	Piano	Handy	
	Who Built de Ark; 1938; 11p	SATB	$c^1 - a^{b2}$	$E^b - f^1$	M	Piano	Handy	
KAY, Ulysses	The Birds; 1969;						Duchess	
	1. The Great Black Crow; 10p	SA	$b^b - f^2$		MD	Piano		
	2. The Skylark; 8p	SA	$g - f^2$		MD	Piano		
	3. The Peacock; 8p	SSA	$a - g^2$		MD	Piano		
	4. The Throstle; 8p	SA	$a^b - f^2$		MD	Piano		
	5. Answer to a Child's Question; 6p	SA	$g - e^2$		MD	Piano		
	Blow, Ye Winds in the Morning (arr.); 1976; pp. 65-77 (Bicentennial Musical Celebration: A Gift from J. C. Penney "Music for Chorus")	SATB	$a - g^2$	$B - f^{\#1}$	E	A Cap	J. C. Penney	
	Choral Triptych; 1967					Organ/solo strings/string orch.		
	1. Give Ear to My Words, O Lord; 19p	SATB	$c^1 - g^{\#2}$	$G - g^1$	D		Asso	A-495
	2. How Long Wilt Thou Forget Me, O Lord; 12p	SATB	$b - g^2$	$G - g^1$	D		Asso	A-496
	3. Alleluia; 16p	SATB	$b - g^{\#2}$	$G - g^1$	D		Asso	A-497
	Christmas Carol; 1957; 7p	SSA	$g - g^2$		M	A Cap	Peer	455-5
	Come Away, Come Away Death; 1954; 5p	TTBB		$G - e^{b1}$	M	A Cap	Peer	ME1014

Composer or Arranger	Title; Copyright Date; Number of Pages	Voicing, Soloist	Vocal Range		Range of Difficulty	A Cappella Accompaniment Instrumentation	Publisher	Catalog Number
			Women	Men				
KAY (continued)	Emily Dickinson Set; 1964; 20p 1. Elysium Is As Far 2. Indian Summer 3. Ample Make This Bed	SSA	$a^b - a^{b2}$		MD	Piano	Leeds	L-472
	The Epicure (from the Cantata "Phoebus Arise"); 1965; 12p	SATB	$b^b - a^{b2}$	$G - g^1$	D	Piano	MCA	L-479
	Epigrams and Hymn; 1975; 20p	SATB	$a - g^{b2}$	$A - g^1$	MD	Organ	Pembroke	PCB-100
	The Flamingo (Pentagraph); 1978; 8p	SA	$a - f^2$		E	Piano	CF	PC1014
	Flowers in the Valley; 1962; 12p	SATB	$b - g^{b2}$	$G^b - g^1$	D	Piano	Peters	P6213
	God the Lord; 1966; 6p	SATB	$b - f^2$	$F - e^1$	E	A Cap	MCA	12616-062
	Grace to You and Peace; 1957; 12p	SATB	$b^b - g^2$	$G - f^1$	MD	Organ	Gray	2467
	How Stands the Glass Around; 1956; 15p	SATB	$b^b - a^{b2}$	$G - f^{\#1}$	MD	A Cap	Asso	A-228
	Hymn-Anthem on the Tune "Hanover"; 1960; 7p	SATB	$g - d^2$	$G - d^1$	E	Organ	Peters	6223
	Inscriptions from Whitman; 1963; 123p	SATB	$c^1 - f^2$		D	Orch.	MS/LC	
	King Arthur (Pentagraph); 1978; 7p	SA	$g - g^{b2}$		E	Piano	CF	PC-1012
	A Lincoln Letter; 1958; 15p	SATB/Bass	$g - g^{b2}$	$E - g^{b1}$	D	A Cap	Peters	6027
	Love Divine (Hymn-Anthem on "Beecher"); 1966; 7p	SATB	$b^b - f^2$	$F - d^1$	E	Organ	MCA	12615-062
	The Miller's Song (Pentagraph); 1978; 8p	SSA	$b - e^2$		E	Piano	CF	PC-1011
	The Monkey's Glue (Pentagraph); 1978; 12p	SSA	$b - f^{\#2}$		E	Piano	CF	PC-1015
	A New Song; 1961;							

Composer or Arranger	Title; Copyright Date; Number of Pages	Voicing, Soloist	Vocal Range Women	Vocal Range Men	Range of Difficulty	A Cappella Accompaniment Instrumentation	Publisher	Catalog Number
KAY (continued)	1. Sing Unto the Lord; 8p	SATB	$b - a^2$	$G - g^1$	M	A Cap	Peters	6136a
	2. Like as a Father; 4p	SATB	$b^b - g^2$	$A^b - e^{b1}$	M	A Cap	Peters	6222a
	3. O Praise the Lord; 6p	SATB	$a^b - g^2$	$A^b - g^1$	M	A Cap	Peters	6229a
	Oh Come, Emmanuel (Hymn-Anthem on "Veni Emmanuel"); 1966; 6p	SATB	$a - d^2$	$G - e^1$	E	Organ	MCA	12613-062
	Parables; 1970; 44p	SATB	$a - g^2$	$G - a^{b1}$	D	Chamber orch.	Duchess	
	1. The Old Arm Chair							
	2. The Hell-Bound Train							
	Phoebus Arise (Cantata); 1960; 177p	SATB			D	Orch.	Belwin	Rental only
	Sally Ann (arr.); 1976; pp. 52–58 (Bicentennial Musical Celebration; A Gift from J. C. Penney "Music for Chorus")	SATB	$b^b - f^2$	$A^b - e^b$	M	A Cap	J. C. Penney	
	Stephen Crane Set; 1972; 54p	SATB			MD	13 players (instrumental)	Duchess	
	Black Riders							
	Mystic Shadow							
	A Spirit							
	War Is Kind							
	Tears, Flow No More (from the Cantata "Phoebus Arise"); 1965; 11p	SSAA/Sop.	$g - g^2$		D	Piano	MCA	L-478
	To Be or Not to Be; 1978; 7p	SSA	$a - f^2$		E	Piano	CF	PC-1013
	To Light That Shines; 1964; 14p	SAB	$a - f^{\#2}$	$c - d^1$	MD	Organ	MCA	L-479
	Triple Set; 1972;						Duchess	
	1. Ode: To the Cuckoo; 10p	TB		$A - g^1$	MD	A Cap		

Composer or Arranger	Title; Copyright Date; Number of Pages	Voicing, Soloist	Vocal Range		Range of Difficulty	A Cappella Accompaniment Instrumentation	Publisher	Catalog Number
			Women	Men				
KAY (continued)	2. Had I a Heart; 6p	TB		$B^b - e^{b1}$	MD	A Cap		
	3. A Toast; 22p	TTBB		$F - g^1$	MD	A Cap		
	Triumvirate; 1954; 33p	TTBB		$E - a^{b1}$	D	A Cap	Peer	ME1013
	1. Music							
	2. The Children's Hour							
	3. The Night March							
	Two Dunbar Lyrics; 1966; 20p	SATB	$g - a^{b2}$	$D - f^1$	M	A Cap	MCA	13404-062
	1. Starry Night; 7p							
	2. Madrigal; 13p							
	A Wreath for Waits; 1956;							
	1. Noel; 10p	SATB	$b^b - a^2$	$A - g^1$	MD	A Cap	Asso	A-209
	2. Lully, Lullay; 10p	SATB	$a - g^2$	$A - f^1$	M	A Cap	Asso	A-210
	3. Welcome Yule; 12p	SATB	$c^1 - a^{b2}$	$B - g^1$	MD	A Cap	Asso	A-211
KERR, Thomas H.	Didn' My Lord Deliver Daniel; 1961; 2p	SATB	$b^b - g^2$	$G - f^1$	M	A Cap	MS	
	Ev'ry Time I Feel da Spirit; 2p	SATB	$c^1 - f^2$	$F - e^{b1}$	E	A Cap	MS	
	Go Tell It on the Mountain; 3p	SATB	$b^b - a^2$	$A - g^{\#1}$	M	A Cap	MS	
	He 'Rose (Easter Spiritual); 1973; 2p	SATB	$c^1 - g^2$	$F - f^1$	M	A Cap	MS	
	I Will Extol Thee; 1942; 6p	SATB	$g^b - g^2$	$A - g^1$	MD	A Cap	MS	
	Nobody Knows; n. d. ; 2p	SATB	$a - e^2$	$F - f^1$	E	A Cap	MS	
	Plen'y Good Room; 1950; 7p	SATB	$g - f^2$	$F - f^1$	MD	A Cap	MS	
	Poor Wayfaring Stranger; 3p	SATB	$g^{\#} - f^{\#2}$	$F^{\#} - f^{\#1}$	MD	A Cap	MS	

Composer or Arranger	Title; Copyright Date; Number of Pages	Voicing, Soloist	Vocal Range		Range of Difficulty	A Cappella Accompaniment Instrumentation	Publisher	Catalog Number
			Women	Men				
KERR (continued)	Prayer for the Soul of Martin Luther King; 14p	SATB	$g^b - b^{b2}$	$G - a^1$	D	A Cap	MS	
	Talk About a Chile; 1954; 8p	SATB	$a - f^{\#2}$	$F^\# - f^{\#1}$	MD	A Cap	MS	
KING, Betty Jackson	Come Down, Angels; 1955; 7p	SATB	$b - f^{\#2}$	$E - f^{\#1}$	E	A Cap	Kjos	ED5393
	Hear de Lambs A-Cryin'; 1961; 4p	SATB	$b^b - g^2$	$G - g^1$	E	A Cap	Kjos	ED5332
	I Couldn't Hear Nobody Pray; 1963; 8p	SATB/Sop.	$g^\# - f^{\#2}$	$E - e^1$	E	A Cap	Kjos	ED5394
	I Want God's Heaven to be Mine; 1973; 6p	SATB/Sop. Ten.	$c^1 - g^2$	$c - f^1$	M	A Cap	Marks	MC4601
	Sinner, Please Don't Let This Harvest Pass; 1978; 7p	SSAATB	$a - a^2$	$A - a^1$	E	A Cap	Mills	2983
	This Little Light of Mine; 1978; 4p	SATB	$b^b - a^{b2}$	$B^b - f^1$	E	A Cap	Hope	HO1812
	Two Christmas Spirituals; 1978; 4p	SATB	$a - f^{\#2}$	$A^b(E^b) - g^{\#1}$	M	A Cap	Somerset	AD1998
	1. Behold That Star Up Yonder 2. Rise Up, Shepherds							
	Wide River; 1961; 4p	SATB	$c^1 - f^2$	$B^b - f^1$	E	A Cap	Kjos	ED5333
LOGAN, Wendell	Hughes Set; 1978; 13p	TTBB			D	A Cap	MS	
	Malcolm, Malcolm; 1977; 11p	SATB	$a - f^2$	$G - e^{b1}$	D	2-channel, half-track stereo tape playback	MS	
	Songs of Our Time; 1969; 69p	SATB			D	Instrumental ensemble	MS	

Composer or Arranger	Title; Copyright Date; Number of Pages	Voicing, Soloist	Vocal Range — Women	Vocal Range — Men	Range of Difficulty	A Cappella Accompaniment Instrumentation	Publisher	Catalog Number
McLIN, Lena	All The Earth Sing Unto The Lord; 1967; 4p	SATB	$g^{\#} - a^2$	$A - g^1$	M	A Cap	Kjos	ED5459
	Cert'nly Lord, Cert'nly Lord; 1967; 12p	SATB	$a^b - b^2$	$B^b - g^1$	M	A Cap	Kjos	ED5458
	Challenge; 1976; 16p	SATB	$b - a^{b2}$	$F - b^{b1}$	E	Piano	Kjos	EDGC-65
	Done Made My Vow to the Lord; 1971; 8p	SATB/Bar.	$a - f^{\#2}$	$F^{\#} - e^1$	E	A Cap	Kjos	ED5872
	Down by the River; 1976; 8p	SATB	$c^1 - g^2$	$G - e^1$	E	A Cap	Kjos	ED5913
	The Earth Is the Lord's; 1969; 8p	SATB	$b - g^2$	$A - g^1$	E	A Cap	Pro Art	2531
	Eucharist of the Soul; 1972; 24p	SATB	$b - f^2$	$G - e^1$	M	Piano/organ	GWM	EDGC41
	For Jesus Christ Is Born; 1971; 3p	SATB	$c^1 - g^2$	$G - d^1$	E	A Cap	Kjos	ED5856
	Free at Last; 1973; 45p	SATB/Sop.	$a - c^3$	$F - a$	MD	Piano	GWM	EDGC39
	Friendship; 1972; 8p	SATB	$b - f^2$	$G - e^1$	MD	Piano	GWM	
	Glory, Glory, Hallelujah; 1966; 8p	SATB	$b - f^{\#2}$	$G - b^{b1}$	E	Piano (op.)	Kjos	ED5430
	Gwendolyn Brooks; 1972; 8p	SATB	$b - e^2$	$G - d^1$	E	Piano	GWM	EDGC21
	If They Ask You Why He Came; 1971; 8p	SATB	$b^b - g^2$	$A^b - e^{b1}$	E	Piano	GWM	EDGC35
	If We Could Exchange Places; 1971; 11p	SATB	$b^b - c^2$	$G - c^1$	M	Flute; electric bass guitar	Marks	4574
	In This World; 1970; 39p	SATB	$g - a^2$	$G - e^1$	M	Piano/cello/electric bass guitar/electric piano	GWM	
	The Little Baby; 1971; 7p	SATB	$a - g^2$	$G - e^1$	E	Piano	Kjos	5855
	The Love of God; 1976; 16p	SATB	$a - e^2$	$F - d^1$	M	Piano	Kjos	EDGC64

Composer or Arranger	Title; Copyright Date; Number of Pages	Voicing, Soloist	Vocal Range Women	Vocal Range Men	Range of Difficulty	A Cappella Accompaniment Instrumentation	Publisher	Catalog Number
McLIN (continued)	Lit'le, Lit'le Lamb; 1959; 8p	SATB/Sop.	b^b – b^2	F – e^{b1}	M	A Cap	Kjos	ED5457
	Memory; 1976; 7p	SATB	b^b – f^2	G – c^1	E	Piano	Kjos	
	My God Is So High; 1972; 7p	SATB	c^1 – g^2	F – e^1	M	A Cap	Kjos	ED5881
	New Born King; 1972; 4p	SATB	c^1 – a^2	F – d^1	E	A Cap	GWM	EDGC23
	Psalm 100; 1961; 7p	SATB	d^1 – a^2	G – f^1	MD	A Cap	Pro Art	2603
	Sanctus and Benedictus; 1971; 4p	SATB	b^b – f^2	F – d^1	M	A Cap	GWM	EDGC34
	Since He Came Into My Life; 1976; 8p	SATB	c^1 – g^2	G – e^1	E	Piano	Kjos	EDGC80
	Te Deum Laudamus; 1976; 11p	SATB	b – f^2	A – d^1	E	Piano/organ	Kjos	EDGC56
	This Land; 1976; 8p	SATB or Unison	g – g^2	G – d^1	E	A Cap	Kjos	EDGC81
	The Torch Has Been Passed; 1971; 11p	SATB	c^1 – a^2	G – f^1	M	A Cap	GWM	EDGC28
	What Will You Put Under Your Christmas Tree; 1971; 8p	SATB	c^1 – a^2	c – e^1	M	A Cap	GWM	EDGC22
	Writ'en Down My Name; 1967; 11p	SATB/Bar.	b – g^2	G – c^1	E	A Cap	Kjos	ED5450
MARGETSON, Edward	Break Forth into Joy; 1936; 16p	SATB	c^1 – g^2	F – g^1	M	Organ	JF	7196
	By the Waters of Babylon; 1932; 12p	SATB	g – g^2	G – a^1	MD	A Cap	GS	7668
	A Christmas Roundelay; 1931; 6p	SATB	b – g^2	$G^\#$ – g^1	MD	A Cap	Gray	1172
	Dark'ning Night the Land Doth Cover; 1937; 11p	SATB/Sop.	a – f^2	F – $f^{\#1}$	M	A Cap	Galaxy	745
	Fair Daffodils, We Weep; 1943; 10p	SATB	a – g^2	A – g^1	MD	A Cap	Boston	2377
	Far from My Heavenly Home; 1932; 8p	SATB	a – a^2	F – $b1$	M	A Cap	JF	6607

Composer or Arranger	Title; Copyright Date; Number of Pages	Voicing, Soloist	Vocal Range Women	Vocal Range Men	Range of Difficulty	A Cappella Accompaniment Instrumentation	Publisher	Catalog Number
MARGETSON (continued)	Hark, Hark, My Soul; 1949; 15p	SATB	$a - g^2$	$F^{\#}(D) - g^1$	M	A Cap	Boston	2556
	He Stooped to Bless; 1936; 4p	SATB	$c^1 - f^2$	$G - g^1$	M	A Cap	JF	7198
	Hosanna, Blessed Is He That Comes; 1945; 4p	SATB	$a - g^2$	$A - g^1$	MD	A Cap	Boston	2550
	Jesus Lives, Alleluia; 1943; 11p	SATB	$a - a^2$	$F - a^1$	M	Organ	Boston	2376
	Lord, What Am I; 1936; 7p	SATB/Sop. Ten.	$a^b - g^2$	$F - a^1$	M	A Cap	Gray	1374
	Morning Hymn of Praise; 1945; 12p	SATB	$b - a^2$	$F - f^1$	M	Organ	Boston	2476
	Now Sleeps the Crimson Petal; 1931; 3p	SATB	$b^b - g^2$	$B^b - g^1$	M	A Cap	JF	6504
	O Come, Let Us Sing; 1935; 16p	SATB	$g^{\#} - g^{\#2}$	$F^{\#} - a^1$	MD	A Cap	JF	6971
	O Mistress Mine; 1931; 5p	SATB	$a - f^{\#2}$	$G - f^{\#1}$	MD	A Cap	JF	6505
	O My Deir Hert, Young Jesus Sweit; 1931; 4p	SSA	$g^{\#} - g^2$		MD	Piano	JF	6555
	O Taste and See; 1936; 11p	SATB	$a - g^2$	$F - f^1$	M	A Cap	JF	7197
	Search Me, O Lord; 1935; 16p	SATB	$a - g^2$	$F^{\#} - g^1$	MD	A Cap	JF	6969
	Sing We a Joyous Measure; 1936; 8p	SATB	$a - g^{\#2}$	$G - f^{\#1}$	M	A Cap	Gray	1409
	Soft Shines the Starlight; 1945; 10p	SATB	$a^b - a^{b2}$	$G - a^{b1}$	M	A Cap	Boston	2551
	Softly Now the Light of Day; 1935; 10p	SATB	$f - a^{b2}$	$F - g^1$	M	A Cap	JF	6972
	A Song for the Chieftain's Son; 1944; 14p	SATB	$a - g^{b2}$	$F - b^1$	MD	A Cap	Boston	2447
	Still, Still with Thee; 1950; 11p	SATB	$a - g^2$	$G - e^1$	M	A Cap	Boston	2746
	Strong Son of God, Immortal; 1946; 12p	SATB	$b^b - g^2$	$F(E^b) - g^1$	M	Organ	Boston	2554
	Through the Day Love; 1944; 7p	SATB	$g - g^2$	$F(E^b) - g^1$	M	Organ	Boston	2451

Composer or Arranger	Title; Copyright Date; Number of Pages	Voicing, Soloist	Vocal Range Women	Vocal Range Men	Range of Difficulty	A Cappella Accompaniment Instrumentation	Publisher	Catalog Number
MARGETSON (continued)	Weep You No More; 1932; 4p	SATB	$b^\flat - g^2$	$G - g^1$	M	A Cap	JF	6606
	Whoso Dwelleth Under the Defence; 1942; 15p	SATB/Sop. Alto; Ten.	$b^\flat - b2$	$G - f^1$	M	Organ	Boston	2365
MAYES, Robert	God Is All There Is; n.d.; 2p	SATB	$a^\flat - a^\flat 2$	$A^\flat - b1$	E	Piano/organ	MS	
	The Ninety-eighth Psalm; 1979; 3p	SATB	$a - g^2$	$G - g^1$	M	Organ	MS	
	Song of Moses; 1980; 3p	SATB/Nar.		$G - g^1$	M	Piano/organ	MS	
	The Twenty-third Psalm; n.d.; 4p	SATB	$b - g^2$	$G - g^1$	M	Piano/organ	MS	
MELLS, Herbert F.	Awake to Righteousness; 1949; 7p	SATB	$b^\flat - a^\flat 2$	$G - f^1$	E	Piano/organ	Handy	
	Behold; 1949; 8p	SATB	$a - f^2$	$F - g^1$	E	A Cap	Handy	
	Bring Along Your Heart; 1951; 7p	TTBB		$G^\flat - g^\flat 1$	E	A Cap	Handy	
	A Christmas Lullaby; 1959; 6p	SATB/Alto Sop.	$b^\flat - f^2$	$E^\flat - f^1$	M	A Cap	Handy	
	Come On Sinner; 1949; 5p	SATB	$b^\flat - a^2$	$G - g^1$	M	A Cap	Handy	
	Go Tell It on the Mountain; 1949; 9p	SATB	$c^1 - a^2$	$d - e^1$	E	A Cap	Handy	
	I Heard the Preaching of the Elders; 1951; 7p	SSAATBB	$b - g^2$	$G - f\#1$	E	A Cap	Birchard	
	I Want to Go to Heaven When I Die; 1950; 8p	SATB	$c^1 - b2$	$A^\flat - f^1$	M	A Cap	Handy	
	I'll Be There; 1952; 9p	SATB	$a - f\#2$	$F\# - f\#1$	M	Piano (op.)	Handy	
	I'm So Glad Trouble Don't Last Always; 1950; 6p	SATB	$a - a^2$	$A - f\#1$	M	A Cap	Handy	
	Let Us Break Bread Together; 1950; 8p	SATB	$a - f^2$	$F - g^1$	M	A Cap	Handy	

Composer or Arranger	Title; Copyright Date; Number of Pages	Voicing, Soloist	Vocal Range (Women)	Vocal Range (Men)	Range of Difficulty	A Cappella Accompaniment Instrumentation	Publisher	Catalog Number
MELLS (continued)	Mine Enchantment; 1950; 7p	SATB	$g - g^{\#2}$	$F^{\#} - f^{\#1}$	M	Piano	Handy	
	My Soul's Been Anchored in the Lord; 1948; 7p	SATB/Sop.	$g^{\#} - g^2$	$A - g^1$	M	A Cap	Handy	
	The Preaching of the Elders; 1949; 8p	TTBB		$E^b - b^1$	M	A Cap	Handy	
	Sometimes I Feel Like a Motherless Child; 1952; 9p	SATB	$g - g^2$	$G - f^1$	M	A Cap	Handy	
	They Crucified My Lord; 1951; 9p	SATB	$a - a^2$	$F^{\#} - f^{\#1}$	M	Piano/organ	Handy	
	They Saw a Star; 1951; 5p	SSAA	$f^{\#} - a^2$		M	Piano/organ	Handy	
	We Are the Men; 1950; 7p	TTBB		$F - f^1$	M	Piano	Handy	
MERRIFIELD, Norman	Ah Done Done; 1942; 6p	TTBB		$A^b - g^1$	E	A Cap	Handy	
	And He Never Said a Mumbling Word; 1972; 8p	SATB	$g - e^2$	$F(E^b) - f^{\#1}$	M	Piano	Rich	MI-72
	Down By the Rivuhside; 1958; 8p	SATB	$b - d^2$	$G - g^1$	M	A Cap	Kjos	5231
	Now Look Away; 1963; 16p	TTBB		$A - f^{\#1}(a^1)$	M	A Cap	Boston	12774
	Remember, O Lord; 1964; 7p	SATB	$a - f^2$	$F - f^1$	M	Piano/organ	Boston	13205
	Show Me Thy Way, O Lord; 1962; 7p	SATB	$b - g^2$	$A - f^{\#1}$	E	Piano/organ	Boston	12733
	Somebody's Knockin' at Yo' Door; 1942; 5p	TTBB		$G - g^1$	M	A Cap	Handy	
	Tryin' to Get Ready; 1968; 8p	SATB	$c^1 - b^2$	$F - f^1$	M	A Cap	Rich	MI-38
MONTAGUE, J. Harold	Joshua Fit de Battle of Jericho; 1935; 8p	SATB	$a - f^2(a^1)$	$F - f^1$	MD	A Cap	WM	W-2811

Composer or Arranger	Title; Copyright Date; Number of Pages	Voicing, Soloist	Vocal Range Women	Vocal Range Men	Range of Difficulty	A Cappella Accompaniment Instrumentation	Publisher	Catalog Number
MONTAGUE (continued)	Let Us Break Bread Together; 1950; 6p	SATB/Sop. Bar.	$c^1 - b^{b2}$	$A^b - f^1$	M	A Cap	Warner	W3408
	Let Us Break Bread Together; 1958; 6p	TTBB		$G^b - g^{b1}$	M	A Cap	WM	9-W3349
	Sinner, Please Don't Let This Harvest Pass; 1937; 8p	SATB	$g^\# - g^{\#2}$	$C^\# - f^{\#1}$	M	A Cap	WM	5-W2915
	Sometimes I Feel Like a Motherless Child; 1958; 6p	SSA/Alto	$g - g^2$		M	Piano	WM	2-W3348
	Swing Low, Sweet Chariot; 1935; 7p	SSA	$f^\# - g^2$		M	Piano	WM	W2838
	Were You There?; 1958; 7p	SATB	$b - g^2$	$G - f^{\#1}$	E	A Cap	WM	5-W3347
	Were You There?; 1950; 7p	TTBB		$E^b - b^1$	M	A Cap	WM	9-23407
MOORE, Carman	Follow Light (In Memory of Texana Paige Franklin); 1977; 14p	SATB/Sop. 2	$f - b^2$	$F - b^1$	MD	Percussion/dbl. bass	MS	
MOORE, Dorothy Rudd	If Music Be the Food of Love (Purcell); 5p	SA	$b - g^2$		E	Piano	Rudmor	
	In Celebration; 1977; 14p	SATB/Sop. Bar.	$a - a^{b2}$	$F - a^1$	MD	Piano	Rudmor	
	Lullaby from Opera "Jocelyn" (Godard); 5p	SA	$b - a^2$		E	Piano	Rudmor	
	Passing By (Purcell); 5p	SSA	$b - e^2$		M	Piano	Rudmor	
	Ride On, King Jesus; 10p	SATB	$b - g^{\#2}$	$B - g^1$	M	Piano	Rudmor	
	This Little Light of Mine; 4p	SATB	$c^1 - f^2$	$A - f^1$	M	A Cap	Rudmor	
	Wiegenlied (Cradle Song, Brahms); 2p	SSA	$b^b - e^2$		E	Piano	Rudmor	

Composer or Arranger	Title; Copyright Date; Number of Pages	Voicing, Soloist	Vocal Range		Range of Difficulty	A Cappella Accompaniment Instrumentation	Publisher	Catalog Number
			Women	Men				
MOORE, Undine Smith	Bound for Canaan's Island; 1960; 7p	SATB	$d^1 - a^2$	$A - g^1$	M	A Cap	Warner	W3653
	Come Along in Jesus Name; 1977; 2p	SATB	$g^\# - g^{\#2}$	$G^\# - e^1$	E	A Cap	Augsburg	11-0558
	Daniel, Daniel Servant of the Lord; 1953; 10p	SATB	$a - a^2$	$F^\# - a^1$	M	A Cap	Warner	W3475
	Fare You Well; 1951; 7p	SATB/Sop. Ten.	$b^b - e^{b2}$	$E^b - b^1$	M	A Cap	WM	W3419
	Glory to God; 1979; 7p	SATB	$a^b - g^2$	$c^b - f^1$	M	A Cap	Augsburg	11-1876
	Hail Warrior; 1957; 8p	SATB	$g - b^2$	$G - a^1$	MD	A Cap	WM	W3544
	I Believe This Is Jesus; 1977; 8p	SATB	$a - a^2$	$A - a^1$	M	A Cap	Augsburg	11-0559
	I Just Come from the Fountain; 1951; 4p	SATB	$a - a^2$	$F^\# - g^1$	E	A Cap	Warner	W3418
	I Would Be True; 1979; 4p	SAB	$c^1 - g^2$	$e^b - e^{b1}$	E	Piano	Augsburg	11-1869
	I'm Going Home; 1978; 7p	SATB/Sop.	$g - a^2$	$F - f^1$	E	A Cap	Augsburg	11-0652
	The Lamb; 1958; 5p	SS or Unison	$c^1 - f^2$		M	Piano	Gray	2531
	Let Us Make Man in Our Image; 1960; 7p	SATB/Sop.	$e - b^2$	$E - a^1$	MD	A Cap	WM	W3652
	Long Fare You Well; 1960; 7p	SATB	$g - a^2$	$G - g^1$	E	A Cap	Augsburg	11-0563
	Lord Have Mercy; 1978; 8p	SATB	$a - a^2$	$G - g^1$	M	A Cap	Augsburg	11-856
	Lord, We Give Thanks to Thee; 1973; 15p	SATB	$g - a^2$	$E^b - g^1$	MD	A Cap	Warner	WB-299
	Mother to Son; 1955; 10p	SATB	$a^b - a^2$	$F - g^1$	M	A Cap	Warner	W3513
	Oh, That Bleeding Lamb; 1977; 7p	SATB	$b - a^2$	$A - f^1$	E	A Cap	Augsburg	11-0557
	Sinner, You Can't Walk My Path; 1958; 6p	SATB	$g - a^2$	$E - g^1$	MD	A Cap	WM	W3546

Composer or Arranger	Title; Copyright Date; Number of Pages	Voicing, Soloist	Vocal Range Women	Vocal Range Men	Range of Difficulty	A Cappella Accompaniment Instrumentation	Publisher	Catalog Number
MOORE (continued)	Striving After God; 1958; 4p	SATB	$a - a^2$	$A - g^1$	M	A Cap	Warner	W3545
	Tambourines to Glory; 1973; 8p	SATB	$a - a^2$	$G - g^1$	M	A Cap	Warner	W3321
	Walk Through the Streets of the City; 1977; 8p	SATB	$a - g^2$	$B - g^1$	M	A Cap	Augsburg	11-0564
	We Shall Walk Through the Valley; 1977; 4p	SATB	$b^b - g^2$	$G - f^1$	E	A Cap	Augsburg	11-0565
	When Susanna Jones Wears Red; 1975; 6p	SATB	$f - a^2$	$E - g^1$	M	A Cap	Warner	CHO795
NICKERSON, Camille	Creole Songs; 1972						Fox	
	1. Aurore Pradere; 6p	SATB	$b - g^2$	$G - e^1$	M	Piano		
	2. Mam'selle Zizi; 6p	SATB	$d^1 - g^2$	$G - e^b$	M	Piano		
	3. Suzanne; 6p	SATB	$b^b - f^2$	$F - f^1$	M	Piano		
	Dear, I Love You; 1946; 14p	SATB	$c^1 - g^2$	$G - g^1$	M	Piano	Boston	2965
	Fais Do-do; 1948; 8p	SSA	$g^\# - g^{\#2}$		M	Piano	Boston	2681
	Gué-Gué Solingaié; 1934; 8p (Creole Folk Lullaby)	SATB	$b - g^2$	$G - e^1$	M	A Cap	Leeds	L-183
PARKER, Reginald	All Over This World; 1967; 7p	SATB	$g - f^2$	$F - f^1$	MD	A Cap	Handy	
	Make a Joyful Noise unto the Lord; 1968; 20p	SATB	$b - a^2$	$A - a^1$	MD	Organ	Handy	
	O God of My Salvation; 1967; 11p	SATB	$b^b - a^2$	$F - g^{\#1}$	M	Organ	D'Lan	

Composer or Arranger	Title; Copyright Date; Number of Pages	Voicing, Soloist	Vocal Range Women	Vocal Range Men	Range of Difficulty	A Cappella Accompaniment Instrumentation	Publisher	Catalog Number
PERKINSON, Coleridge-Taylor	Fredome-Freedom; 1970; 40p	SATB	$c^1 - c^3$	$F - g^1$	D	Piano	Tosci	T-101
PERRY, Julia	Carillon Heigh-Ho; 1947; 8p	SATB	$b - g^2$	$G - g^1$	M	A Cap	CF	CM6318
	Song of Our Savior; 1953; 8p	SATB	$a - f\#^2$	$F\# - e^1$	M	A Cap	Galaxy	1946
	Ye, Who Seek the Truth; 1952; 7p	SATB/Ten.	$c - c^2$	$A - b1$	E	Organ	Galaxy	1901
PITTMAN, Evelyn La Rue	Any How; 1952; 3p	SATB	$b^b - a^{b2}$	$F - e^{b1}$	E	A Cap	CF	CM6692
	Joshua; 1955; 15p	SATB/Alto Bar.	$g^\# - e^2$	$E - e^1$	MD	Piano	CF	CM6780
	Nobody Knows de Trouble I See; 1954; 7p	SATB/Sop.	$b - g^2$	$G - f^{\#1}$	M	A Cap	CF	CM6650
	Rocka Mah Soul; 1952; 11p	SATB/Bar.	$c^1 - e^2$	$G - e^1$	M	A Cap	CF	CM6650
	Sit Down Servant; 1949; 8p	SATB/Bar.	$b - g^2$	$F - e^{b1}$	E	A Cap	CF	CM6527
PRICE, Florence	Heav'n-Bound Soldier; 1949; 4p	SSA	$g - e^2$		E	Piano	Handy	
PRICE, John E.	Amen; 1954; 6p	SATB/2 Choirs	$a^b - b^{b2}$	$D - a$	MD	A Cap	SSP	
	Barely Time to Study Jesus (3rd version); 1977; 54p	SATB/Sop. 7 Readers			D	Percussion	SSP	
	Carol II; 1962; 4p	Unison			E	A Cap	SSP	
	Carol III; (O Lord We Want to Thank You); 1969; 9p	SATB/Contralto	$a - g^{\#2}$	$F - g^1$	M	A Cap	SSP	
	Damnation of Doctor Faustus; 1962; 79p	SATB/Ten.			D	Small orch.	SSP	

Composer or Arranger	Title; Copyright Date; Number of Pages	Voicing, Soloist	Vocal Range Women	Vocal Range Men	Range of Difficulty	A Cappella Accompaniment Instrumentation	Publisher	Catalog Number
PRICE (continued)	Dona Nobis Pacem; 1972; 7p	SATB	c - g²	G - f¹	M	A Cap	SSP	
	Magnificat Anima Mea Dominum; 1954; 7p	SATB	b♭ - b²	A♭ - b1	MD	A Cap	SSP	
	"Mist"; 1962; 4p	SATB	a - b²	D# - a1	MD	A Cap	SSP	
	The Patience That Outlasts Chains-- Part I; 1969; 16p	SATB Sounds, Singing			D	3 Speakers, percussion, harp	SSP	
	Prayer: Martin Luther King; 1970; 11p	SATB/Bar.	g - a²	F# - g¹	D	A Cap	SSP	
	Psalm 117; 1967; 3p	SATB	g - a²	G - f#¹	D	A Cap	SSP	
	Rounds for the 12th Month; 1978; 9p 1. The Baby 2. The Man 3. Mary 4. The Mystery 5. Jesus Will Not Return 6. Humanity: First in Africa					A Cap	SSP	
	A Sketch; 1959; 3p	SATB	g - a b2	F - f¹	M	A Cap/3 flutes, 1 oboe	SSP	
	Song of the Liberty Bell; n.d.; 103p	SATB/Nars. /Solos			D	Instrumental/ Tape	SSP	
	Two "Jesus Pieces"; 1958; 9p	SATB	f - a b2	E♭ - g¹	MD	A Cap	SSP	
	What Month Was Jesus Born In?; 1970; 31p	SATB	g - d²	A - e¹	M	B♭ Clar., 2 guitars, piano, drum set	SSP	
REECE, Cortez	Mary Had a Baby; 1959; 1978; 7p	SATB/Sop.	b♭ - g²	G - e b1	M	A Cap	Hinshaw	HMC-316

Composer or Arranger	Title; Copyright Date; Number of Pages	Voicing, Soloist	Vocal Range		Range of Difficulty	A Cappella Accompaniment Instrumentation	Publisher	Catalog Number
			Women	Men				
RIVERS, Clarence	Anamnesis; 1972; 3p (Two Alternate Settings)	Unison/SATB	$c^1 - g^2$	$F - g^1$	E	Piano	Stimuli	
	Bless the Lord; 1972; 7p (Two Settings)	Unison/SATB	$e - g^2$	$G - d^1$	E	Piano	Stimuli	
	Five Different Amens; 1970; 9p (Nine Settings)	Unison/SATB	$a - a^2(d^3)$	$F^\# - g^1$	MD	Piano	Stimuli	
	Freedom; 1973; 8p	SATB	$c^1 - g^2$	$G - e^1$	E	Piano	Stimuli	
	God Is Love; 1972; 11p (Two Settings)	Unison/SATB	$g - b^{b2}$	$C - e^1$	E	Piano	Stimuli	
	Like a Dry Land; 1972; 9p (Three Settings)	Unison/SATB	$b - e^2$	$A - e^1$	M	Piano	Stimuli	
	Mass Dedicated to the Brotherhood of Man; 1966; 59p	Unison/SATB			M	A Cap	Stimuli	
	My God Is So High; 1970; 5p	Unison/SATB	$c - f^2$	$A^b(F) - e^1$	E	Piano	Stimuli	
	Our Father; 1972; 7p	Unison/SATB	$a - c^2$	$c - e^1$	E	Piano	Stimuli	
	Prayer of St. Francis; 1970; 12p	Unison/SATB	$a - d^2$	$A - e^1$	E	Piano	Stimuli	
	Resurrection; 1972; 27p	Unison/SATB	$a - g^2$	$G - g^1$	M	Piano	Stimuli	
	Ride On, King Jesus; 1970; 7p (Three Settings)	Unison/SATB	$c^1 - a^2$	$F - f^1$	M	Piano	Stimuli	
	Sing a Song unto the Lord; 1972; 10p (Two Settings)	Unison/SATB	$b^{b1} - a^{b2}$	$G - g^1$	E	Piano	Stimuli	
	Take Away Our Hearts of Stone; 1972; 5p (Four Settings)	Unison/SATB	$b^b - c^3$	$F - f^1$	E	Piano	Stimuli	
	That We May Live; 1972; 5p	Unison/SATB	$b^b - g^2$	$G - c^{b1}$	E	Piano	Stimuli	
	There Is None Like Him; 1972; 5p	Unison/SATB	$c^1 - f^2$	$F - d^1$	E	Piano	Stimuli	

Composer or Arranger	Title; Copyright Date; Number of Pages	Voicing, Soloist	Vocal Range Women	Vocal Range Men	Range of Difficulty	A Cappella Accompaniment Instrumentation	Publisher	Catalog Number
RIVERS (continued)	Toward One Goal; 1972; 7p (Three Settings)	Unison/SATB	b^b - g^2	E^b - b1	M	Piano	Stimuli	
	Trisagion; 1970; 3p (Two Settings)	Unison/SATB	b - g^2	G - g^1	E	Piano	Stimuli	
	Witness of Christ; 1972; 15p	SATB	d^1 - $b2$	B^b - $f^{\#}1$	M	Piano	Stimuli	
ROBERTS, Howard	Beulah Land; 1972; 12p	SATB	b^b - $f^{\#}2$	F - $f^{\#}1$	E	Drums/shaker	LG	51691
	I Want Jesus to Walk with Me; 1970; 8p	SATB	e^1 - f^2	G(D) - f^1	E	A Cap/drums	LG	51572
	Let My People Go; 1970; 7p	SATB	c^1 - e^2	A - e^1	MD	A Cap/drums	LG	51556
	Motherless Child; 1970; 8p	SATB	c^1 - g^2	F - e^1	M	A Cap/shaker, drums	LG	51559
	Sinner Man; 1970; 12p	SATB/Sop.	b - g^2	F - a	MD	A Cap/drums	LG	51571
	Soon I Will Be Done; 1970; 8p	SATB/Sop.	c^1 - f^2	G(D) - f^1	M	A Cap	LG	51558
	Steal Away; 1970; 7p	SATB	$c^{\#}1$ - f^2	F(E) - f^1	M	A Cap/drums	LG	51554
	Talk About a Child; 1970; 6p	SATB	c^1 - f^2	$F^{\#}$ - f^1	M	A Cap/drums	LG	51555
ROBINSON, Alphonse	Soliloquy to a Martyred Hero (A Trilogy, Op. 22); 1978; 45p (Written in cooperation with the late Betty McConnell Brewster of Denver)	SATB			MD	Full orch.	MS	
ROBINSON, Josephus	Don't Let Nobody Turn You Around; 1948; 7p	SATB	a - f^2	F - d^1	E	A Cap	Robinson	
	Give Me That Old Time Religion; 1947; 7p	SATB	b - e^2	G - e^1	E	A Cap	Robinson	
	He That Believe; 1948; 5p	SATB	b - d^2	B^b - e^1	E	A Cap	Robinson	

Composer or Arranger	Title; Copyright Date; Number of Pages	Voicing, Soloist	Vocal Range Women	Vocal Range Men	Range of Difficulty	A Cappella Accompaniment Instrumentation	Publisher	Catalog Number
ROBINSON (continued)	I'm Leaning on the Lord; 1947; 8p	SATB	$a - e^2$	$G - c^1$	E	A Cap	Robinson	
	I've Been Changed; 1948; 7p	SATB	$a - f^2$	$F - f^1$	E	A Cap	Robinson	
	Old Ship of Zion; 1947; 5p	SATB	$b^b - f^2$	$B^b - f^1$	E	A Cap	Robinson	
	The River of Jordan; 1948; 9p	SATB	$g - g^2$	$E - f^1$	M	A Cap	Robinson	
ROXBURY, Ronald Marle	As Dew in Aprille; 1972; 6p	SATB	$d^1 - f^{\#2}$	$A - f^1$	MD	A Cap	Walton	3503
	Ave Maria; 1972; 6p	SATB	$a - g^1$	$G - g^1$	D	A Cap	Walton	3504
	That Yonge Child; 1974; 4p	SATB	$b - g^2$	$F^{\#} - f^1$	MD	A Cap	Walton	2253
	There Is No Rose of Such Vertu; 1972; 6p	SATB	$c^{\#1} - e^2$	$A - f^{\#}$	M	A Cap	Walton	3505
RYDER, Noah	An' I Cry; 1939; 7p	SATB	$g - g^2$	$G - e^1$	E	A Cap	Handy	
	Balm in Gilead; 1938; 5p	SATB/Ten.	$c^1 - f^2$	$F - g^1$	M	A Cap	Handy	
	Bethlehem Lullaby; 1946; 1p	SATB/Sop.	$c^1 - c^2$	$C - c^1$	E	A Cap	Row	401
	By and By; 1938; 5p	SATB	$g - g^2$	$E^b - b1$	E	A Cap	Handy	
	Done Paid My Vow; 1938; 9p	SATB	$a - a^2$	$E - g^1$	M	A Cap	Handy	
	Don't Be Weary Traveler; 1939; 6p	SATB/Alto	$g - b2$	$E^b - g^1$	E	A Cap	Handy	
	Gonna Journey Away; 1939; 8p	SATB/Alto	$d^1 - d^2$	$F - f^1$	M	A Cap	Handy	
	Great Day' 1938; 5p	SATB	$b - a^2$	$F - f^1$	M	A Cap	Handy	
	Gwine Up; 1936; 5p	SATB/Bar.	$d^1 - e^2$	$A - g^1$	E	A Cap	Handy	
	He Ain't Coming Here to Die; 1949; 7p	SATB/Alto	$b^b - d^2$	$B^b - b^b$	E	A Cap/piano (op.)	JF	8441

Composer or Arranger	Title; Copyright Date; Number of Pages	Voicing, Soloist	Vocal Range Women	Vocal Range Men	Range of Difficulty	A Cappella Accompaniment Instrumentation	Publisher	Catalog Number
RYDER (continued)	Hear the Lambs a Crying; 1938; 5p	SATB	$a - e^2$	$E - f^1$	E	A Cap	Handy	
	I Got a Mother in Heaven; 1938; 5p	SATB/Bar.	$c^1 - g^2$	$G - e^1$	E	A Cap	Handy	
	I Heard the Preaching of the Elders; 1938; 7p	SATB	$c - g^2$	$E - g^1$	M	A Cap	Handy	
	I Will Never Betray My Lord; 1935; 5p	SATB	$g - f^2$	$F - d^1$	M	A Cap	Handy	
	In Bright Mansions Above; 1939; 6p	SATB	$a - g^2$	$F - g^1$	E	A Cap	Handy	
	Joshua Fought the Battle of Jericho; 1946; 4p	TTBB		$F^\# - g^1$	M	A Cap	Row	506
	Let Us Break Bread Together; 1945; 4p	SATB	$b - g^2$	$G - e^1$	E	A Cap	JF	FECS117
	Let Us Break Bread Together; 1965; 4p	SAB	$a - f^2$	$G - d^1$	E	Piano/organ	JF	9557
	Let Us Break Bread Together; 1958; 3p	SSA	$g - g^2$		E	A Cap	JF	9065
	Let Us Break Bread Together; 1950; 3p	TTBB		$G - a^1$	E	A Cap	JF	8514
	Little David Play On Your Harp; 1947; 6p	TTBB		$G - g^1$	E	Piano	Row	505
	Little David Play On Your Harp; 1947; 6p	SSA	$g - g^2$		E	A Cap/piano (op.)	Row	601
	Lord I Want to Be a Christian; 1938; 5p	SATB	$b^b - e^{b2}$	$E^b - e^{b1}$	E	A Cap	Handy	
	Love Song; 1946; 4p	TTBB		$A^b - a^{b1}$	E	A Cap (op.)	Row	363
	Mary Borned a Baby; Bethlehem Lullaby; 1946; 4p	SATB/Sop.	$c^1 - e^{b2}$	$A^b - e^{b1}$	E	A Cap	Row	401
	A Mighty Fortress Is Our God; 1947; 7p	TTBB		$F - g^1$	M	A Cap	Row	R370
	My Lord Is So High; 1939; 8p	SATB	$b^b - g^2$	$B^b - a^1$	E	A Cap	Handy	

Composer or Arranger	Title; Copyright Date; Number of Pages	Voicing, Soloist	Vocal Range		Range of Difficulty	A Cappella Accompaniment Instrumentation	Publisher	Catalog Number
			Women	Men				
RYDER (continued)	My Soul Doth Magnify the Lord; 1948; 6p	SATB/Sop.	$b^b - f^2$	$B^b - e^1$	E	Piano/organ	JF	9072
	Nobody Knows de Trouble I See; 1938; 4p	SATB	$b - d^2$	$G - d^1$	E	A Cap	Handy	
	No More Auction Block; 1939; 4p	SATB/Sop.	$g - e^2$	$G(D) - d^1$	E	A Cap	Handy	
	O Lem'me Shine; 1936; 5p	SATB/Bar.	$c\#^1 - d^2$	$G - g^1$	E	A Cap	Handy	
	Run to Jesus; 1936; 7p	SATB/Bar.	$g - c^2$	$G - d^1$	E	A Cap	Handy	
	Sea Suite for Male Voices; 1946; 11p	TTBB		$F - a^1$	M	A Cap	Handy	
	See That Babe in the Lowly Manger; 1946; 11p	TTBB		$G - g^1$	E	A Cap	GS	9550
	Sunrise; 1939; 8p	SATB	$a - a^2$	$A - f^1$	M	A Cap	Handy	
	Them Dry Bones; 1947; 6p	TTBB/Bass		$A^b - e^{b1}$	E	A Cap	Row	504
	This Ol' Hammer; 1947; 9p	TTBB		$F - f^1$	M	A Cap	GS	9635
	Who'll Be a Witness; 1947; 12p	TTBB		$A^b - e^{b1}$	E	A Cap	GS	9650
SIMPSON, Eugene Thamon	Hold On; 1974; 13p	SATB	$g - a^2$	$F - f^1$	M	A Cap	Murbo	979
	Nobody Knows de Trouble I've Seen; 1976; 3p	SATB	$a - a^2$	$F - d^1$	E	A Cap	Bourne	
	Sinnuh, Please Don't Let Dis Harves' Pass; 1976; 11p	SATB	$a - a^2$	$G - g^1$	M	A Cap	Bourne	
	Steal Away; 1975; 6p	SATB	$a - d^{b2}$	$A^b - e^1$	E	A Cap	Bourne	
	True Religion; 1977; 5p	SATB	$a - g^2$	$F - g^1$	E	A Cap	Bourne	

Composer or Arranger	Title; Copyright Date; Number of Pages	Voicing, Soloist	Vocal Range Women	Vocal Range Men	Range of Difficulty	A Cappella Accompaniment Instrumentation	Publisher	Catalog Number
SMITH, Hale	Comes Tomorrow: A Jazz Cantata; 1972; rev. 1976; 66p	SATB			MD		To be pub. by Presser	
	In Memoriam--Beryl Rubinstein; 1959; 16p	SATB	b - a^2	A$^\#$ - g^1	D	Chamber orch.	Galaxy	HP56
	Toussaint L'Ouverture--1803; 1977; 14p	SATB	b^b - g^2	F$^\#$ - e	MD	Piano	Presser	342-40126
	Two Kids; 1973; 10p	SATB	b^b - a^{b2}	F - a^{b1}	MD	A Cap	Marks	MC4594
SMITH, William H.	Cheer the Weary Traveler; 1937; 4p	SATB	g - e^2	G - e^1	E	A Cap	Kjos	1004
	Children Don't Get Weary; 1937; 4p	SATB	b - g^2	G - e^1	E	A Cap	Kjos	1007
	Climbin' Up the Mountain; 1937; 4p	SATB	e^b - e^{b2}	A^b - e^{b1}	E	A Cap	Kjos	1001
	Climbin' Up the Mountain; 1937; 6p	TTBB		E^b - f^1 (ab1)	M	A Cap	Kjos	1101
	Didn't My Lord Deliver Daniel; 1938; 8p	SATB	c^1 - b^2	F - f^1	E	A Cap	Kjos	1014
	Everytime I Feel the Spirit; 1937; 4p	SATB	a - f$^{\#2}$	A - f$^{\#1}$	M	A Cap	Kjos	1006
	Goin' to Heaven Anyhow; 1937; 4p	SATB	b^b - e^{b2}	E^b - f^1	M	A Cap	Kjos	1009
	Good News; 1937; 4p	SATB	e^{b1} - d^{b2}	A^b - g^1	E	A Cap	Kjos	1005
	Go Tell It on the Mountain; 1937; 4p	SATB	a - f^2	F - f^1	E	A Cap	Kjos	1010
	I Couldn't Hear Nobody Pray; 1937; 2p	SATB/Sop. Ten.	b^b - a^2	F - f^1	E	A Cap	Kjos	1011
	Plenty Good Room; 1937; 6p	SATB	b - g^2(b^2)	G - f$^{\#1}$	M	A Cap	Kjos	1003
	Ride the Chariot; 1939; 8p	SATB	c^1 - g^2(b^2)	G - d^1(g^1)	M	A Cap	Kjos	1015
	Ride the Chariot; 1939; 8p	TTBB/Ten.		G - g^1	M	A Cap	Kjos	1102

Composer or Arranger	Title; Copyright Date; Number of Pages	Voicing, Soloist	Vocal Range Women	Vocal Range Men	Range of Difficulty	A Cappella Accompaniment Instrumentation	Publisher	Catalog Number
SMITH (continued)	Sometimes I Feel Like a Motherless Child; 1939; 8p	SATB/Alto or Bar. Sop. or Ten.	$a - a^2$	$A - f^1$	M	Organ/piano	Kjos	1013
	Sometimes I Feel Like a Motherless Child; 1937; 3p	TTBB/Sop.		$G - f^1$	E	A Cap	Kjos	1113
SOUTHALL, Mitchell	The Blind Man Stood on the Road and Cried; 1960; 8p	TTBB		$G - g^1$	M	A Cap	Jusko	J-207
	The Blind Man Stood on the Road and Cried; 1960; 8p	SATB	$b - g^2$	$G - f^1$	M	A Cap	Jusko	J-205
	The Blind Man Stood on the Road and Cried; 1960; 8p	SSAA	$g - g^2$		M	A Cap	Jusko	J-206
	I Want Jesus to Walk with Me; 1960; 8p	SSA/Sop.	$g - d^{b2}$		E	A Cap	Jusko	J-170
	I Want Jesus to Walk with Me; 1960; 10p	SATB/Sop.	$a^b - e^{b2}$	$F - f^1$	M	A Cap	Jusko	J-208
	I Want Jesus to Walk with Me; 1960; 8p	TTBB/Ten.		$F - g^1$	E	A Cap	Jusko	J-210
	In Silent Night; 1957; 5p	SATB	$g - d^2$	$G - d^1$	M	A Cap	Jusko	J-105
	Joshua Fit de Battle of Jericho; 1959; 12p	TTBB		$A - a^1$	MD	A Cap	Jusko	J-211
	Nobody Knows the Trouble I've Seen; 1960; 7p	SATB	$c^1 - f^2$	$F - f^1$	M	A Cap	Jusko	J-209
	Nobody Knows the Trouble I've Seen; 1960; 8p	SSA	$f - f^2$		M	A Cap	Jusko	J-209
	Sometimes I Feel Like a Motherless Child; 1959; 4p	SATB	$g - g^2$	$E - g^1$	M	A Cap	CF	9167
	Steal Away; 1959; 7p	SATB	$a - e^2$	$E^b - g^1$	E	A Cap	Jusko	J-212

Composer or Arranger	Title; Copyright Date; Number of Pages	Voicing, Soloist	Vocal Range — Women	Vocal Range — Men	Range of Difficulty	A Cappella Accompaniment Instrumentation	Publisher	Catalog Number
SOUTHALL (continued)	There's No Hiding Place Down There; 1959; 11p	SATB	$a^b - g^2$	$F - f^1$	M	A Cap	Jusko	J-213
	Wade in de Waters; 1957; 7p	SATB/Sop.	$f - f^2$	$F - d^{b1}$	MD	Piano (op.)	Handy	
STILL, William Grant	And They Lynched Him on a Tree; 1961; 46p	SATB/Contralto; nar.		$A^b - e$	MD	Full orch.	JF	
	The Blind Man; 1977; 6p	SATB	$g - e^{b2}$	$A^b - b1$	M	Piano	Gemini	GP-406
	Christmas in the Western World; 1967; 44p (Narration by Verna Arvey) 1. A Maiden Was Adoring God, the Lord 2. Ven, Nino Divino 3. Aquinaldo 4. Jesous Ahatonhia 5. Tell Me, Shepherdess 6. De Virgen Mary Had a Baby Boy 7. Los Reyes Magos 8. La Pinata 9. Glad Christmas Bells 10. Sing! Shout! Tell the Story	SATB			M	Piano/string quartet/string orch.	Southern	
	Ev'ry Time I Feel the Spirit; 1977; 7p	SATB	$b - f^2$	$G - f^1$	E	Piano	Gemini	GP-405
	Hard Trials (from "Three Rhythmic Spirituals"); 1961; 8p	SATB	$c^1 - f^2$	$c - f^1$	M	Piano	Bourne	808
	Here's One; 1941; 8p	SATB/Sop.	$a - e^2$	$B - f^{\#1}$	M	A Cap	Presser	322-40037
	I Feel Like My Time Ain't Long; 1956; 4p	SATB	$c^1 - f^2$	$c - d^1$	E	A Cap	Presser	312-40304
	Is There Anybody Here; 1956; 4p	SATB	$c^1 - e^2$	$c - e^1$	E	Piano	Presser	312-40305

Composer or Arranger	Title; Copyright Date; Number of Pages	Voicing, Soloist	Vocal Range		Range of Difficulty	A Cappella Accompaniment Instrumentation	Publisher	Catalog Number
			Women	Men				
STILL (continued)	Lawd, Ah Wants to Be a Christian; 1938; 5p	SATB	$d^1 - g^2$	$G - a^1$	M	Piano	Handy	
	Lord, I Looked Down the Road (from "Three Rhythmic Spirituals"); 1961; 11p	SATB/Sop. Ten.	$a - f^2$	$d - f^{\#1}$	M	Piano	Bourne	807
	Toward Distant Shores; 1977; 7p	SATB	$a^b - g^2$	$F - g^1$	M	Piano	Broude	GP-407
	Victory Tide; 1952; 8p	SATB	$c^1 - a^2$	$G - a^1$	M	Piano	JF	7831
	The Voice of the Lord (Psalm XXIX); 1956; 10p	SATB/Ten.	$b - a^2$	$A - g^{\#1}$	M	Organ	Witmark	5-W3273
STOR, Jean	Four and Twenty Elders; 1937; 11p	SATB	$c^1 - g^2$	$G - e^1$	M	Piano	Handy	
	God Is Our Salvation; 1948; 7p	SATB	$a - a^{b2}$	$A^b - a^1$	M	Piano	Handy	
	Going to Hold Out to the End; 1936; 10p	SATB	$g - a^2$	$F - f^1$	M	Piano	Handy	
	Hold the Wind; 1933; 10p	SATB	$b - g^{b2}$	$G - a^{b1}$	M	Piano	Handy	
	I Want Jesus to Walk with Me; 1933; 9p	SATB/Sop. / Bar.	$g - f^2$	$D - f^1$	MD	Piano	Handy	
	My Way Is Cloudy; 1933; 7p	SATB	$a - g^2$	$F - g^1$	M	Piano	Handy	
	One Hundred Thirty-seventh Psalm; 1948; 7p	SATB	$b - g^2$	$G - f^{\#}$	E	Piano	Handy	
	Pale Horse and Rider; 1936; 11p	SATB/Mez. Ten.	$c^1 - a^2$	$F - f^1$	M	Piano	Handy	
	Sit Down; 1933; 11p	SATB	$c^1 - a^{b2}$	$F - a^{b1}$	M	Piano	Handy	
	The Kingdoms of Our Lord; 1948; 7p	SATB	$c^{\#1} - g^2$	$A - a^1$	M	Piano	Handy	
	The Lord's Prayer; 1948; 5p	SATB	$c^1 - a^2$	$G - g^1$	E	Piano	Handy	

Composer or Arranger	Title; Copyright Date; Number of Pages	Voicing, Soloist	Vocal Range Women	Vocal Range Men	Range of Difficulty	A Cappella Accompaniment Instrumentation	Publisher	Catalog Number
STOR (continued)	The Waters of Life; 1948; 9p	SATB	$b - a^2$	$E^b - f^\#$	E	Piano	Handy	
SWANSON, Howard	Nightingales; 1952; 11p	TTBB		$G - a^1$	MD	A Cap	WT	
	We Delighted, My Friend; 13p	SATB	$g - b^{b2}$	$G - g^1$	MD	A Cap	WT (MS)	
TAYLOR, Maude	How Beautiful upon the Mountains; 1964; 7p	SATB/Sop. Ten.	$b - g^2$	$G - f^{\#1}$	M	Piano/organ	Handy	
	I Will Lift Up Mine Eyes; 1961; 8p	SATB	$a - f^2$	$A - f^1$	M	Piano	Boston	12613
	They Shall Run and Not Be Weary; 1960; 9p	SATB/Ten.	$a - f^2$	$F - f^1$	E	Piano/organ	Elkan	HE-168
TILLIS, Frederick C.	Alleluia; 1969; 28p	SATB	$g - g^2$	$E - g^1$	MD	A Cap	ACA	
	Five Spirituals; 1976; 81p	SATB/Sop.	$a - b^{b2}$	$G^b - a^1$	D	Brass Choir	ACA	
	Freedom; 1974; 31p	SATB	$a - g^2$	$G - g^1$	D	A Cap	Southern	
	Halleluyah; 1966; 15p	TTBB		$F - b^1$	MD	A Cap	ACA	
	Seasons; 1973;							
	1. Spring; 5p	SSA	$a - f^2$		M	A Cap	MS	
	2. Summer; 22p	SSA	speaking		M	Tambourine, African "thumb piano"		
	3. Autumn; 10p	SSA	$b^b - g^2$		MD	Gong, cymbals, cluster bells, wood block		
	4. Winter; 16p	SSA	$a - a^2$		MD	Cello		
WALKER, George	Give Thanks unto the Lord; 1975; 14p	SSA	$a - g^{\#2}$		MD	Organ	GM	

Composer or Arranger	Title; Copyright Date; Number of Pages	Voicing, Soloist	Vocal Range		Range of Difficulty	A Cappella Accompaniment Instrumentation	Publisher	Catalog Number
			Women	Men				
WALKER (continued)	Gloria in Memoriam; 1963; 10p	SSA	$f^\# - f^{\#2}$		MD	Organ	NV	
	Mass; 63p; 1979	SATB/Sop. Alto; Ten. Bass			D	Orch. (Piano reduction)	GM	
	O Lord God of Hosts; 1975; 12p	SATB	$c^{\#1} - g^2$	$G - a^1$	MD	Organ	GM	
	O Praise the Lord; 1975; 14p	SATB	$a - e^2$	$G - g^1$	M	A Cap	GM	
	Praise Ye the Lord; 1975; 9p	SATB	$b^\# - g^2$	$A - a^{b1}$	MD	Organ	GM	
	Sing unto the Lord; 1975; 12p	SATB	$b - a^2$	$A - a^1$	MD	A Cap	GM	
	Stars; 1968; 6p	SATB	$b^b - g^2$	$B - e^1$	MD	A Cap	Asso	A-596
	Three Lyrics for Chorus; 1971;	SATB						
	1. The Bereaved Maid; 8p		$b^b - f^2$	$F - f^1$	M	Piano	GM	
	2. Take, O Take Those Lips Away; 7p		$b^b - c^2$	$G - f^1$	M	Piano	GM	
	3. O Western Wind; 8p		$b - g^{\#2}$	$C^\# - f^{\#1}$	MD	Piano	GM	
	With This Small Key; 1975; 11p	SATB	$g - a^2$	$G - a^{\#1}$	D	A Cap	GM	
WHALUM, Wendell	Amazin' Grace; 1973; 11p	SATB/Sop.	$b^b - g^2$	$G - f^1$	E	Organ	LG	51750
	Give Me Jesus; 1978; 7p	SATB	$a^b - g^2$	$D^b - f^1$	M	A Cap	GS	52039
	Mary Was the Queen of Galilee; 1974; 10p	SATB/Sop.	$a - g^2$	$G - a^1$	M	A Cap	LG	51808
	My Lord, What a Morning; 1979; 10p	TTBB/Bar.		$G - a^1$	M	A Cap	LG	51917
	Roberta Lee; 1975; 11p	TTBB/Ten.		$F - a(b^1)$	M	A Cap	LG	51866
	Somebody's Calling My Name; 1975; 11p	TTBB		$F - a^{b1}$	M	A Cap	LG	51932

Composer or Arranger	Title; Copyright Date; Number of Pages	Voicing, Soloist	Vocal Range — Women	Vocal Range — Men	Range of Difficulty	A Cappella Accompaniment Instrumentation	Publisher	Catalog Number
WHALUM (continued)	Sweet Home; 1975; 11p	SATB/Sop.	a^b–f^2	A^b–f^1	E	A Cap	LG	51869
	You'd Better Run; 1976; 11p	TTBB/Bar.		A^b–b^1	M	A Cap	LG	51749
WHITE, Clarence	Blow, Gabriel; 1937; 8p	TTBB/Bar.		E–a^1	M	A Cap	CF	CM2212
	Dis Train; 1949; 5p	SATB	b–f^2	G–d^1	M	Piano	Fox	PS 42
	Dis Train; 1959; 5p	TTBB		A–g^1	M	A Cap	Fox	PS 49
	Down By de Ribber Side; 1930; 5p	SATB/Solo quartet	c^1–f^2	A^b–f^1	E	A Cap	CF	4542
	Great Day; 1937; 11p	SATB	a–a^2	F–a^1	MD	A Cap	CF	CM4606
	Hear the Good News; 1961; 7p	TTBB		G–g^1	M	Piano	Colombo	NY1929
	Heritage; 1960; 35p	SATB	a^b–b^2	c–g^1	MD	Orch.	PC	
	I Know I Have Another Building; 1935; 11p	SATB	a–f^2	F–f^1	M	A Cap	Presser	21217
	I'm Goin' Home; 1930;	SATB	b–e^2	G–e^1	E	A Cap	CF	4543
	In That Great Gettin' Up Morning; 1940; 2p	SATB	b–g^2	A^b–e^1	E	A Cap	CF	28854-20
	Lonesome Valley; 1951; 5p	SATB	a–f^2	F–c^1	M	A Cap	Fox	PS66
	Nobody Knows de Trouble I've Seen; 1924; 6p	SATB	b–d^2	G–g^1	M	Piano	CF	4520
	Search My Heart; 1952; 4p	SATB	d^1–f^2	G–b^1	M	A Cap	CA	S119
	Sinner, Please Don't Let This Harvest Pass; 1935; 11p	SATB	$f^{\#}$–e^2	E–g^1	MD	A Cap	Presser	1935
	Somebody's Knocking at Your Door; 1955; 6p	SATB	a^b–g^2	E^b–b^1	M	A Cap	CA	R144

Composer or Arranger	Title; Copyright Date; Number of Pages	Voicing, Soloist	Vocal Range		Range of Difficulty	A Cappella Accompaniment Instrumentation	Publisher	Catalog Number
			Women	Men				
WHITE (continued)	This Old Hammer; 1961; 5p	TTBB		E^b - g^1	M	A Cap	Colombo	NY1928
	Wide River; 1938; 5p	SATB/Sop.	a – f^2	F – f^1	M	A Cap	CF	4635
WILLIAMS, Arnold K.	The Dreams I Dreamed; 1972; 5p	SA	b^b – f^2		E	Piano	Ply	JR-508
	Give Me Jesus; 1972; 14p	SATB/Sop.	a – g^2($b2$)	G – g^1	M	A Cap	Ply	JR-160
	Hallelujah; 1970; 11p	SATB	b^b – $a^{\#2}$ ($b2$)	G – g^1	M	A Cap	Ply	JR-148
	Just a Closer Walk with Thee; 1972; 9p	SATB/Sop. Ten.	$b^\#$ – a^2	A – $f^{\#1}$	M	Piano	Ply	JR-162
	My Lord's Always Near; 1970; 11p	SATB/Sop.	a – g^2 ($bb2$)	F – f^1	M	A Cap	Ply	JR-150
	When My Savior; 1972; 7p	SATB/Ten. Sop.	a – a^2	G – $f^{\#1}$	E	A Cap	Ply	JR-159
WILLIAMS, Henry	He Gives A-Plenty for Them All; 1967; 11p	SATB	b^b – f^2	A^b – d^1	M	A Cap	Williams	
	He Is the King of Kings; 1966; 8p	SATB	g – g^2	F – c^1	E	A Cap	Williams	
	I Will Praise Him; 1966; 10p	SATB	c^1 – g^2	G – e^1	M	A Cap	Williams	
	I Will Sing; 1964; 4p	SATB	b – g^2	G – e^1	E	A Cap	Williams	
	Talking 'Bout Your Servant; 1966; 7p	SATB/Sop.	a – a^2	G – d^1	E	A Cap	Williams	
WILLIAMS, Julius P., Jr.	Christmas Fantasy; 1977; 5p	SATB	c^1 – f^2	F – e^1	E	Piano (op.)	MS	
	In Commendation of Music; n.d.; 11p	SATB	a^b – c^3	F – g^1	MD	Piano	MS	
	Soon A' Will Be Done; 1978; 8p	SATB	b – a^2	B – $f^{\#1}$	E	A Cap	MS	

Composer or Arranger	Title; Copyright Date; Number of Pages	Voicing, Soloist	Vocal Range Women	Vocal Range Men	Range of Difficulty	A Cappella Accompaniment Instrumentation	Publisher	Catalog Number
WILSON, Olly	In Memoriam: Martin Luther King, Jr.; 1968; 24p	SATB	g – b♭2	E♭ – b1	D	Tape	MS	
WORK, John Wesley, III	The Angels Done Bowed Down; 1943; 7p	SATB/SATB	c1 – f2	F – d♭1	M	A Cap	Presser	21515
	Danse Africaine; 1951; 15p	SATB	b♭ – a♭2	G – f1	M	Piano/drums, tamb., triangle	Smith	
	Do Not I Love Thee, O My Lord; 1960; 8p	SATB/Sop.	a♭ – g2	G – f1	M	Organ	Presser	312-4000
	Done Made My Vow to the Lord; 1956; 8p	SATB/Sop. Ten.	g# – g2	B – f#1	E	A Cap	Galaxy	2110
	For the Beauty of the Earth; 1936; 8p	SATB	c1 – g2	G – f1		Organ	JF	6851
	Give Me Your Hand; 1960; 10p	SATB/Sop.	a – g#2	E – g#1	M	A Cap	Mills	399
	Glory to That New Born King; 1935; 7p	SATB/Sop.	c1 – c2	G – e♭1	E	A Cap	Presser	312-21208
	Glory to That New Born King; 1935; 7p	SATB/Sop.	c1 – g2	G – g1	M	A Cap	Presser	312-2120
	Go Tell It on the Mountain; 1953; 7p	SA/Sop.	a – d2		E	Piano	Galaxy	1960
	Go Tell It on the Mountain; 1953; 7p	SSA/Sop.	a – d2		M	Piano	Galaxy	1.1753.1
	Go Tell It on the Mountain; 1946; 11p	TTBB/Ten.		A♭(E♭) – f1	M	A Cap	Galaxy	1.583.1
	Go Tell It on the Mountain; 1945; 11p	SATB/Sop. Ten.	g – f2	F – c1	M	A Cap	Galaxy	GMC1532
	Going Home to Live with God; 1934; 8p	SATB/Sop.	b♭ – a♭2	F – a1	MD	A Cap	JF	6794
	Golgotha Is a Mountain; 1959; 9p	SATB	a – f2	G – g1	E	Piano/organ	Galaxy	GMC2155
	Grigi, Grigi; 1953; 11p	SATB/Sop.	g – g2	G – f1	M	A Cap	Galaxy	1962

Composer or Arranger	Title; Copyright Date; Number of Pages	Voicing, Soloist	Vocal Range		Range of Difficulty	A Cappella Accompaniment Instrumentation	Publisher	Catalog Number
			Women	Men				
WORK (continued)	How Beautiful upon the Mountains; 1934; 8p	SATB	– g^2	$F - f^1$	M	A Cap	Galaxy	GM633
	I Got a House in Baltimore; 1953; 15p	TTBB/Ten.		$F^{\#} - a^1$	M	A Cap	Galaxy	1964
	I, John, Saw the Holy Number; 1962; 8p	SATB	$c^{\#1} - a^2$	$F^{\#} - g^1$	M	A Cap	Galaxy	GMC2236
	Isaac Watts Contemplates the Cross (Choral Cycle); 1962;							
	1. When I Survey the Wondrous Cross; 13p	SATB	$d^1 - g^2$	$A - f^1$	M	Piano	BR	4561-15
	2. Alas, and Did My Savior Bleed; 10p	SATB/Ten.	$c^1 - g^2$	$B - e^1$	M	Piano	BR	4561-16
	3. T'was on That Dark, Doleful Night; 8p	SATB/Bar.	$c^1 - g^2$	$A - f^1$	M	Piano	BR	4561-17
	4. How Condescending and How Kind; 7p	SATB/Sop.	$b^b - b$	$G - d^1$	M	Piano	BR	4561-18
	5. Now for a Tune of Lofty Praise; 10p	SATB	$b - a^2$	$G - g^1$	E	Piano	BR	4561-19
	6. Hosanna to the Prince of Light; 9p	SATB/Alto Ten.; Bar.	$c^{\#} - a^2$	$A - e^1$	E	Piano	BR	4561-20
	I've Known Rivers; 1955; 12p	SATB	$g^{\#} - a^2$	$F^{\#} - g^1$	MD	A Cap	Galaxy	GMC20751
	I've Known Rivers; 1955; 12p	SSAATTBB	$g^{\#} - g^{\#2}$	$F^{\#} - g^1$	M	A Cap	Galaxy	2075
	Jesus, Lay Your Head in the Window; 1960; 12p	SATB/Sop. Ten.	$c^1 - a^2$	$c - g^1$	M	A Cap	Galaxy	GMC2166
	John, Saw the Holy Number; 1962; 8p	SATB/Sop.	$c^1 - a^2$	$F - g^1$	M	A Cap	Galaxy	GMC2236
	The Joys of Mary; 1956; 19p	SATB/Bar.	$b^b - g^2$	$E - g^1$	M	A Cap	Elkan	1104
	Jubilee (Collection of 10 Negro Spirituals); 1962; 62p	SATB					Holt, Rinehart Winston	

Composer or Arranger	Title; Copyright Date; Number of Pages	Voicing, Soloist	Vocal Range		Range of Difficulty	A Cappella Accompaniment Instrumentation	Publisher	Catalog Number
			Women	Men				
WORK (continued)	Listen to the Angels Shouting; 1947; 4p	SSA or SAA	$a - a^2$		M	A Cap	Galaxy	1649
	Little Black Train; 1956; 15p	SATB/Mez.	$b - f^{\#2}$	$E - e^1$	M	A Cap	Galaxy	2088
	Lord, I'm Out Here on Your Word; 1952; 13p	SATB/Sop. Ten.	$a^b - g^{b2}$	$A^b - d^{b1}$	M	A Cap	Galaxy	1903
	My Lord, What a Mornin'; 1964; 4p	SATB/Bar. Sop.	$b^b - e^{b2}$	$G^b - g^{b1}$	E	A Cap	Presser	312-40622
	New Born; 1945; 11p	SSATTB/Sop.	$g - f^2$	$E^b - a^{b1}$	M	A Cap	JF	8119
	Po' Ol' Laz'rus; 1931; 11p	TTBB/Ten. Bass		$E^b - e^{b1}$	M	A Cap	JF	6513
	Railroad Bill; 1950; 11p	TTBB/Bar.		$G^\# - g^{\#1}$	M	Piano	Galaxy	1802
	Rock, Mount Sinai; 1962; 8p	SATB	$a - e^2$	$G - f^1$	M	A Cap	Galaxy	2237
	Rockin' Jerusalem; 1940; 11p	SATB/Sop. Ten.	$e^1 - e^2$	$A - d^1$	M	A Cap	Presser	312-21427
	The Singers (Cantata); 1949; 23p	SATB/Bar.	$d^{b1} - a^2$	$A - a^1$	M	Orch./piano	Mills	
	Sinner Please Don't Let This Harvest Pass; 1952; 11p	SATB/Sop.	$g - a^{b2}$	$F - b^{b1}$	M	A Cap	Presser	322-40020
	The Sun Himself Shall Fade; 1951; 8p	SATB/Alto	$b - g^2$	$A - e^1$	M	Piano/organ	Galaxy	1848
	There's a Meeting Here Tonight; 1950; 14p	TTBB		$F - f^1$	MD	A Cap	ECS	2150
	This Little Light o' Mine; 1973; 7p	SATB/Sop.	$g^\# - e^2$	$F^\# - e^1$	M	A Cap	Galaxy	1.1384
	This Ol' Hammer; 1933; 16p	TTBB/Ten.		$G - g^1$	M	A Cap	Galaxy	629
	Wasn't That a Mighty Day; 1934; 7p	SATB/Ten.	$d^1 - f^2$	$F(D) - g^1$	M	A Cap	JF	6835
	Wasn't That a Mighty Day; 1934; 7p	SSA	$c^1 - f^2$		M	Piano	JF	FE6845

Composer or Arranger	Title; Copyright Date; Number of Pages	Voicing, Soloist	Vocal Range		Range of Difficulty	A Cappella Accompaniment Instrumentation	Publisher	Catalog Number
			Women	Men				
WORK (continued)	'Way Over in Egypt Land; 1947; 11p	SATB	$a^b - a2$	$F - f^1$	M	A Cap	Galaxy	1574
	You May Bury Me in the East; 1950; 9p	TTBB/Ten.		$F^\# - f^{\#1}$	M	A Cap	ECS	2149

TITLE INDEX

79

Any How .... Pittman, Evelyn La Rue

Any Human to Another .... Baker, David

Aquinaldo (from Christmas in the Western World) .... Still, William Grant

As by the Streams of Babylon .... Dett, R. Nathaniel

As Dew in Aprille .... Roxbury, Ronald

As the Hart Panteth (SATB) .... Fax, Mark

As the Hart Panteth (SAB) .... Fax, Mark

Ask for the Old Poets .... Dett, R. Nathaniel

Aurore Pradere (from Creole Songs) .... Nickerson, Camille

Autumn (from Seasons) .... Tillis, Frederick

Ave Maria .... Dett, R. Nathaniel

Ave Maria .... Furman, James

Ave Maria .... Roxbury, Ronald

Awake to Righteousness .... Mells, Herbert F.

Ay, Ay, Ay .... De Paur, Leonard

Babe Is Born, A .... Hancock, Eugene

Baby Bethlehem .... Boatner, Edward

Ballad of the Brown King, The (from The Christmas Cantata) .... Bonds, Margaret

Balm in Gilead .... Ryder, Noah

Band of Angels .... Hairston, Jester

Barely Time to Study Jesus .... Price, John

Battle, The .... Hailstork, Adolphus, III

Beatitudes, The .... Cooper, William B.

Before the Sun Goes Down (arr. of Londonderry Air) .... Dawson, William L.

Behold .... Mells, Herbert F.

Behold That Star .... Burleigh, Harry T.

Behold That Star Up Yonder .... King, Betty Jackson

Behold the Star .... Dawson, William L.

Benedictus .... Harris, Robert A.

Bereaved Maid (from Three Lyrics for Chorus) .... Walker, George

Bethlehem Lullaby .... Ryder, Noah

Better Be Ready .... Dett, R. Nathaniel

Beulah Land .... Roberts, Howard

Birds, The .... Kay, Ulysses

Black Children (from Five Songs to the Survival of Black Children) . Baker, David

Bless the Lord .... Rivers, Clarence J.

Blest Be the Tie .... Coleman, Charles

Blind Man, The .... Still, William Grant

Blind Man Stood on the Road and Cried, The .... Clary, Salone

Blind Man Stood on the Road and Cried, The (SATB) .... Southall, Mitchell B.

Christmas Fantasy	Williams, Julius, Jr.
Christmas Gift (SATB)	Hairston, Jester
Christmas Gift (SSAB)	Hairston, Jester
Christmas in de Tropics	Hairston, Jester
Christmas in the Western World	Still, William Grant
Christmas Lullaby, A	Mells, Herbert F.
Christmas Roundelay, A	Margetson, Edward
City Called Heaven	Johnson, Hall
City of God	Dett, R. Nathaniel
Climbin' Up the Mountain (SATB)	Smith, William H.
Climbin' Up the Mountain (TTBB)	Smith, William H.
Cloths of Heaven, The	Hailstork, Adolphus, III
Collect for Peace, A	Harris, Robert A.
Come Along in Jesus Name	Moore, Undine
Come Away, Come Away Death	Kay, Ulysses
Come Down, Angels	King, Betty Jackson
Come Here, Lord	Hancock, Eugene W.
Come On Sinner	Mells, Herbert F.
Come Thou Long Expected Jesus	Furman, James
Comes Tomorrow: A Jazz Cantata	Smith, Hale
Communion	Dett, R. Nathaniel
Communion Service	Harris, Robert A.
Couldn't Hear Nobody Pray	Burleigh, Harry T.
Counterpoint	Da Costa, Noel
Creation, De	Burleigh, Harry T.
Creole Songs	Nickerson, Camille
Crucifixion	Hairston, Jester
Crucifixion (SATB)	Johnson, Hall
Crucifixion (TTBB)	Johnson, Hall
Crucifixion, The	Boatner, Edward
Damnation of Doctor Faustus	Price, John E.
Daniel, Daniel Servant of the Lord	Moore, Undine
Danse Africaine	Work, John W., III
Dark'ning Night the Land Doth Cover	Margetson, Edward
Dear, I Love You	Nickerson, Camille
Deep River	Burleigh, Harry T.
Deep River	Dett, R. Nathaniel
Deep River	Hairston, Jester
Deliverance	Hall, Frederick
Dere's No Hidin' Place Down Dere	Johnson, Hall

Eucharist of the Soul	McLin, Lena
Everytime I Feel the Spirit	Billups, Kenneth
Everytime I Feel the Spirit	Smith, William H.
Ev'ry Time I Feel de Spirit	Burleigh, Harry T.
Ev'ry Time I Feel the Spirit (SATB)	Dawson, William L.
Ev'ry Time I Feel the Spirit (SSA)	Dawson, William L.
Ev'ry Time I Feel the Spirit (TTBB)	Dawson, William L.
Ev'ry Time I Feel the Spirit	Dett, R. Nathaniel
Ev'ry Time I Feel the Spirit	Fax, Mark
Ev'ry Time I Feel the Spirit	Kerr, Thomas H., Jr.
Ev'ry Time I Feel the Spirit	Still, William Grant
Except the Lord Build This House	Fax, Mark
Ezek'el Saw the Wheel	Bonds, Margaret
Ezekiel Saw de Wheel (SATB)	Burleigh, Harry T.
Ezekiel Saw de Wheel (SSA)	Burleigh, Harry T.
Ezekiel Saw de Wheel	Dawson, William L.
Fair Daffodils, We Weep	Margetson, Edward
Fais Do-do	Nickerson, Camille
Faith Unlocks the Door	Hairston, Jester
Fanfare - "Noel"	Curtis, Marvin
Far from My Heavenly Home	Margetson, Edward
Fare You Well	Moore, Undine
Fatuous Tragedy, A	Burleigh, Harry T.
Feed-A My Sheep (SATB)	Dawson, William L.
Feed-A My Sheep (SSA)	Dawson, William L.
Feed-A My Sheep (TTBB)	Dawson, William L.
Five Choral Responses	Carter, Roland
Five Different Amens	Rivers, Clarence
'Five/Seven'	Da Costa, Noel
Five Songs to the Survival of Black Children	Baker, David
Five Spirituals	Tillis, Frederick
Fix Me, Jesus	Johnson, Hall
Flamingo, The (from Pentagraph)	Kay, Ulysses
Flowers in the Valley	Kay, Ulysses
Follow Light	Moore, Carman
For Jesus Christ Is Born	McLin, Lena
For the Beauty of the Earth	Harris, Robert A.
For the Beauty of the Earth	Work, John W., III
Four and Twenty Elders	Stor, Jean
Four Little Foxes	Furman, James

Go Tell It on the Mountain	Smith, William H.
Go Tell It on the Mountain (SATB)	Work, John W., III
Go Tell It on the Mountain (SSA)	Work, John W., III
Go Tell It on the Mountain (SA)	Work, John W., III
Go Tell It on the Mountain (TTBB)	Work, John W., III
God Is All There Is	Mayes, Robert
God Is Love (two alt. settings)	Rivers, Clarence
God Is Our Salvation	Stor, Jean
God Rest Ye Merry, Gentlemen	De Paur, Leonard
God the Lord (Hymn-Anthem)	Kay, Ulysses
God's Goin' Buil' Up Zion's Wall	Hairston, Jester
Goin' Down Dat Lonesome Road	Hairston, Jester
Goin' to Heaven Anyhow	Smith, William H.
Goin' to Hold Out to the End	Stor, Jean
Going Home to Live with God	Work, John W., III
Golgotha Is a Mountain	Work, John W., III
Gonna Journey Away	Ryder, Noah
Good Evening, Mrs. Flanagan	De Paur, Leonard
Good News	Smith, William H.
Goodbye Song	Hairston, Jester
Gospel Train, De	Burleigh, Harry T.
Gossip, Gossip	Hairston, Jester
Grace to You and Peace	Kay, Ulysses
Great Black Crow, The (from The Birds)	Kay, Ulysses
Great Day	Ryder, Noah
Great Day	White, Clarence
Great God A'Mighty	Hairston, Jester
Grigi, Grigi	Work, John W., III
Gué-Gué Solingaié	Nickerson, Camille
Gwendolyn Brooks	McLin, Lena
Gwine Up	Ryder, Noah
Had I a Heart (from Triple Set)	Kay, Ulysses
Hail Mary (SATB)	Dawson, William L.
Hail Mary (TTBB)	Dawson, William L.
Hail the Crown: Old Negro Melody	Fax, Mark
Hail Warrior	Moore, Undine
Hallelujah	Fax, Mark
Hallelujah	Williams, Arnold K.
Halleluyah	Tillis, Frederick
Hand Me Down	Hairston, Jester

Honor! Honor! (SSA)	Johnson, Hall
Honor! Honor! (SATB)	Johnson, Hall
Honor! Honor! (TTBB)	Johnson, Hall
Hope Thou in God	Fax, Mark
Hosanna, Blessed Is He That Comes	Margetson, Edward
Hosanna to the Prince of Light (from Isaac Watts Contemplates the Cross)	Work, John W., III
Hosanna to the Son of David	Adams, Leslie
How Beautiful upon the Mountain	Taylor, Maude C.
How Beautiful upon the Mountains	Work, John W., III
How Condescending and How Kind (from Isaac Watts Contemplates the Cross)	Work, John W., III
How Long Wilt Thou Forget Me, O Lord (from Choral Triptych)	Kay, Ulysses
How Stands the Glass Around?	Kay, Ulysses
Hughes Set	Logan, Wendell
Hymn-Anthem on the Tune "Hanover" (O Worship the King)	Kay, Ulysses
I Ain't Gonna Study War No More	Johnson, J. Rosamond
I Believe This Is Jesus	Moore, Undine
I Belong to That Band	Jessye, Eva
I Can Tell the World	Hairston, Jester
I Cannot Stay Here By Myself	Johnson, Hall
I Couldn't Hear Nobody Pray	Hicks, L'Roy
I Couldn't Hear Nobody Pray	King, Betty Jackson
I Couldn't Hear Nobody Pray	Smith, William H.
I Dream a World	Baker, David
I Feel Like My Time Ain't Long	Still, William Grant
I Got a House in Baltimore	Work, John W., III
I Got a Mother in Heaven	Ryder, Noah
I Got a Mule	Johnson, Hall
I Got Shoes	Johnson, Hall
I Have a Dream	Da Costa, Noel
I Have a Dream	Fax, Mark
I Have a Dream (Oratorio)	Furman, James
I Heard the Preaching of the Elders	Mells, Herbert F.
I Heard the Preaching of the Elders	Ryder, Noah
I Hope My Mother Will Be There	Burleigh, Harry T.
I, John, Saw the Holy Number	Work, John W., III
I Just Come from the Fountain	Moore, Undine
I Know I Have Another Building	White, Clarence
I Shall Pass Through This World	Bonds, Margaret
I Stood on the River of Jordan	Billups, Kenneth

In Celebration	Moore, Dorothy Rudd
In Commendation of Music	Williams, Julius, Jr.
In Dat Great Gettin' Up Mornin'	Hairston, Jester
In His Care-O (SATB)	Dawson, William L.
In His Care-O (TTBB)	Dawson, William L.
In Memoriam	Hailstork, Adolphus, III
In Memoriam--Beryl Rubinstein	Smith, Hale
In Memoriam: Martin Luther King, Jr.	Wilson, Olly
In My Father's House Are Many Mansions	Fax, Mark
In Silent Night	Southall, Mitchell
In That Great Gettin'-Up Mornin'	White, Clarence
In This World	McLin, Lena
Inscriptions from Whitman (Cantata)	Kay, Ulysses
Introit and Gradual for Easter Day	Hancock, Eugene
Is There Anybody Here	Still, William Grant
Isaac Watts Contemplates the Cross (Choral Cycle)	Work, John W., III
It's All over Me	Hairston, Jester
I've Been 'Buked	Boatner, Edward
I've Been 'Buked	Johnson, Hall
I've Been Changed	Robinson, Josephus
I've Been in de Storm So Long	Burleigh, Harry T.
I've Heard of a City Called Heaven	Handy, W. C.
I've Known Rivers (SATB)	Work, John W., III
I've Known Rivers (SSAATTBB)	Work, John W., III
Jerry	De Paur, Leonard
Jesous Ahatonhia (from Christmas in the Western World)	Still, William Grant
Jesus Hung and Died	De Paur, Leonard
Jesus, Lay Your Head in de Winder	Johnson, Hall
Jesus, Lay Your Head in the Window	Work, John W., III
Jesus Lives, Alleluia	Margetson, Edward
Jesus Walked This Lonesome Valley (SATB)	Dawson, William L.
Jesus Walked This Lonesome Valley (TTBB)	Dawson, William L.
John, Saw the Holy Number	Work, John W., III
Joshua	Pittman, Evelyn La Rue
Joshua Fit de Battle o' Jericho	Johnson, J. Rosamond
Joshua Fit de Battle of Jericho	Hairston, Jester
Joshua Fit de Battle of Jericho	Montague, J. Harold
Joshua Fit de Battle of Jericho	Southall, Mitchell
Joshua Fought the Battle of Jericho	Ryder, Noah

Lincoln Letter, A	Kay, Ulysses
Listen to the Angels Shouting	Work, John W., III
Listen to the Lambs	Dett, R. Nathaniel
Lit'l' Boy-Chile	Dawson, William L.
Lit'le, Lit'le Lamb	McLin, Lena
Little Baby, The	McLin, Lena
Little Black Train	Work, John W., III
Little David, Play on Your Harp	Hairston, Jester
Little David Play on Your Harp (SATB)	Ryder, Noah
Little David Play on Your Harp (SSA)	Ryder, Noah
Little David Play on Your Harp (TTBB)	Ryder, Noah
Little Lamb	Da Costa, Noel
Little Love, A (from Harlem Suite)	Cunningham, Arthur
Little Mother of Mine	Burleigh, Harry T.
Live-a Humble	Hairston, Jester
Lonesome Valley	White, Clarence
Long Fare You Well	Moore, Undine
Lord, Have Mercy	Moore, Undine
Lord, I Can't Stay Away	Boatner, Edward
Lord, I Don't Feel No-Ways Tired	Johnson, Hall
Lord, I Looked Down the Road (from Three Rhythmic Spirituals)	Still, William Grant
Lord, I Want to Be a Christian	Johnson, Hall
Lord, I Want to Be a Christian	Ryder, Noah
Lord, I'm Out Here on Your Word	Work, John W., III
Lord Is My Light, The	Fax, Mark
Lord Jesus Think on Me	Hancock, Eugene
Lord, Look Down (from Two Prayers)	Cunningham, Arthur
Lord Tryeth the Heart, The	Gregory, Percy
Lord, We Give Thanks to Thee	Moore, Undine
Lord, What Am I	Margetson, Edward
Lord's Prayer, The	Coleman, Charles
Lord's Prayer, The	Stor, Jean
Love Divine	Kay, Ulysses
Love of God, The	McLin, Lena
Love Song	Adams, Leslie
Love Song	Ryder, Noah
Lullaby from Opera "Jocelyn" (Godard)	Moore, Dorothy Rudd
Lully, Lullay (from A Wreath for Waits)	Kay, Ulysses
Madrigal	Adams, Leslie

Madrigal (from Two Dunbar Lyrics)	Kay, Ulysses
Magnificat Anima Mea Dominum	Price, John E.
Maiden Was Adoring God, A (from Christmas in the Western World)	Still, William Grant
Make a Joyful Noise	Fax, Mark
Make a Joyful Noise unto the Lord	Parker, Reginald
Malcolm, Malcolm	Logan, Wendell
Mam'selle Zizi (from Creole Songs)	Nickerson, Camille
Man from Nazareth	Boatner, Edward
Mango Walk	Clark, Rogie
Marry a Woman Uglier Than You	De Paur, Leonard
Mary Borned a Baby	Ryder, Noah
Mary Had a Baby (SATB)	Dawson, William L.
Mary Had a Baby (TTBB)	Dawson, William L.
Mary Had a Baby	Johnson, Hall
Mary Had a Baby	Reece, Cortez
Mary, Mary, Where Is Your Baby	Hairston, Jester
Mary Was the Queen of Galilee	Whalum, Wendell
Mary's Little Baby	Davis, Elmer
Mary's Little Boy Chile	Hairston, Jester
Mass	Hancock, Eugene
Mass	Walker, George
Mass Dedicated to the Brotherhood of Man	Rivers, Clarence
Mass for Choir and Congregation	Cooper, William B.
Mass of the Poor	Cooper, William B.
Mass of the Poor (Deep River-arr.)	Cooper, William B.
Mass to St. Philip (Festival Mass of Thanksgiving)	Cooper, William B.
May the Grace of Christ Our Saviour	Harris, Robert A.
Memory	McLin, Lena
Mighty Fortress Is Our God, A	Ryder, Noah
Miller's Song, The (from Pentagraph)	Kay, Ulysses
Mine Enchantment	Mells, Herbert F.
"Mist"	Price, John E.
Mister Banjo	Burleigh, Harry T.
Mister Banjo	Nickerson, Camille
Monkey's Glue, The (from Pentagraph)	Kay, Ulysses
Mornin'	Hairston, Jester
Morning Hymn of Praise	Margetson, Edward
Mother to Son	Moore, Undine
Motherless Child	Roberts, Howard
Mourn Not the Dead	Hailstork, Adolphus, III
Move! Let Me Shine!	Jessye, Eva

Munday Man (from Harlem Suite)	Cunningham, Arthur
Music (from Triumvirate)	Kay, Ulysses
Music for Services for Trial Use	Hancock, Eugene
Music in the Mine	Dett, R. Nathaniel
Music When Soft Voices Die	Childs, John
My God Is So High	McLin, Lena
My God Is So High	Rivers, Clarence J.
My Lord Is So High	Ryder, Noah
My Lord, What a Mornin'	Burleigh, Harry T.
My Lord, What a Mornin'	Work, John W., III
My Lord What a Morning	Whalum, Wendell
My Lord What a Mourning	Dawson, William L.
My Lord's Always Near	Williams, Arnold K.
My Name Is Toil	Hailstork, Adolphus, III
My Soul Doth Magnify the Lord	Ryder, Noah
My Soul Is a Witness	Billups, Kenneth
My Soul's Been Anchored in the Lord	Mells, Herbert F.
My Spirit on Thy Care	Archer, Dudley
My Way Is Cloudy	Stor, Jean
My Way's Cloudy	Dett, R. Nathaniel
Negro Bell Carol	James, Willis Laurence
Negro Speaks of Rivers, The	Bonds, Margaret
New Born	Work, John W., III
New Born Again	Billups, Kenneth
New Born King	McLin, Lena
New Song, A	Kay, Ulysses
Nightingales	Swanson, Howard
Night's March, The	Kay, Ulysses
Ninety-eighth Psalm, The	Mayes, Robert
No More Auction Block	Ryder, Noah
No Ne Li Domi	Hairston, Jester
Nobody Knows	Kerr, Thomas H., Jr.
Nobody Knows de Trouble I See	De Paur, Leonard
Nobody Knows de Trouble I See	Ryder, Noah
Nobody Knows de Trouble I See	Pittman, Evelyn La Rue
Nobody Knows de Trouble I've Seen	Simpson, Eugene
Nobody Knows de Trouble I've Seen	White, Clarence
Nobody Knows the Trouble I See	Burleigh, Harry T.

Oh! Freedom!	Johnson, Hall
Oh! Holy Lord	Hairston, Jester
Oh, Holy Lord	Johnson, Hall
Oh Lord, Have Mercy on Me	Johnson, Hall
Oh, Po' Little Jesus	De Paur, Leonard
Oh, Po' Little Jesus	James, Willis Laurence
Oh, Rock-a My Soul	Hairston, Jester
Oh, That Bleeding Lamb	Moore, Undine
Oh, What a Beautiful City	Boatner, Edward
Oh, What a Beautiful City	Dawson, William L.
Old Ark, The	Clark, Rogie
Old Arm Chair, The (from Parables)	Kay, Ulysses
Old Ship of Zion	Robinson, Josephus
Old Southern Melody	Fax, Mark
On a Drop of Dew	Cooper, William B.
On Ma Journey	Boatner, Edward
One Hundred and Thirty-seventh Psalm	Stor, Jean
Opportunity	Handy, W. C.
Ordering of Moses, The (Oratorio)	Dett, R. Nathaniel
Our Father	Rivers, Clarence
Our Troubles Was Hard	Hairston, Jester
Out in the Fields (SSA)	Dawson, William L.
Out in the Fields (SATB)	Dawson, William L.
Out of the Depths	Fax, Mark
Pale Horse and Rider	Stor, Jean
Palm Sunday Anthem, A	Hancock, Eugene
Parables	Kay, Ulysses
Passing By (Purcell)	Moore, Dorothy Rudd
Patience That Outlasts Chains--Part I	Price, John E.
Pauline, Pauline	De Paur, Leonard
Peacock (from The Birds)	Kay, Ulysses
Personals (Cantata)	Anderson, T. J.
Phoebus Arise (Cantata)	Kay, Ulysses
Pinata, La (from Christmas in the Western World)	Still, William Grant
Plenty Good Room	Smith, William H.
Plen'y Good Room	Kerr, Thomas H., Jr.
Po' Ol' Laz'rus	Work, John W., III
Poem of America	Fax, Mark
Poor Man Lazrus (SSA)	Hairston, Jester
Poor Man Lazrus (SATB)	Hairston, Jester

Ride the Chariot (SATB)	Smith, William H.
Ride the Chariot (TTBB)	Smith, William H.
Ring de Christmas Bells	Hairston, Jester
Rise Up, Shepherd and Foller	Hairston, Jester
Rise Up, Shepherd and Follow (SATB)	Dett, R. Nathaniel
Rise Up, Shepherd and Follow (TTBB)	Dett, R. Nathaniel
Rise Up Shepherd and Follow	Fax, Mark
Rise Up, Shepherds	King, Betty Jackson
River Chant	Johnson, Hall
River of Jordan, The	Robinson, Josephus
Roberta Lee	Whalum, Wendell, and James, Willis Laurence
Rock Mt. Sinai!	Jessye, Eva
Rock, Mount Sinai	Work, John W., III
Rocka Mah Soul	Pittman, Evelyn La Rue
Rockin' Jerusalem	Work, John W., III
Roll Jordan Roll	Gillum, Ruth H.
Roun' de Glory Manger	James, Willis Laurence
'Round the Glory Manger	Fax, Mark
Rounds for the 12th Month	Price, John
Royal Banners Forward Go, The (for Palm Sunday)	Cooper, William B.
Rugged Yank, The	Dawson, William L.
Run Li'l' Chillun	Johnson, Hall
Run to Jesus	Ryder, Noah
Saint Louis Blues (SATB)	Handy, W. C.
Saint Louis Blues (SA or TB)	Handy, W. C.
Saint Louis Blues (SSA or TTB)	Handy, W. C.
Sakura Sakura	Hairston, Jester
Sally Ann	Kay, Ulysses
Salve Regina	Furman, James
Salve Salvage in the Spin (from Five Spirituals)	Tillis, Frederick
Same Train	Johnson, J. Rosamond
Sanctus and Benedictus	McLin, Lena
Scandalize My Name	Burleigh, Harry T.
Scandalize My Name	Johnson, Hall
Sea Suite for Male Voices	Ryder, Noah
Search Me, O Lord	Margetson, Edward
Search My Heart	White, Clarence
Seasons	Tillis, Frederick
See That Babe in the Lowly Manger	Ryder, Noah
Seeking for That City	Coleman, Charles

Somebody's Calling My Name	Whalum, Wendell
Somebody's Knockin' at Yo' Door	Merrifield, Norman
Somebody's Knocking at Your Door (SATB)	Dett, R. Nathaniel
Somebody's Knocking at Your Door (SSA)	Dett, R. Nathaniel
Somebody's Knocking at Your Door	White, Clarence
Sometimes I Feel Like a Motherless Child	Burleigh, Harry T.
Sometimes I Feel Like a Motherless Child	Hairston, Jester
Sometimes I Feel Like a Motherless Child	Johnson, Hall
Sometimes I Feel Like a Motherless Child	Mells, Herbert F.
Sometimes I Feel Like a Motherless Child	Montague, J. Harold
Sometimes I Feel Like a Motherless Child	Southall, Mitchell
Sometimes I Feel Like a Motherless Child (SATB)	Smith, William H.
Sometimes I Feel Like a Motherless Child (TTBB)	Smith, William H.
Son of Mary	Dett, R. Nathaniel
Song for the Chieftain's Son, A	Margetson, Edward
Song of Creation, A	Hancock, Eugene
Song of Moses	Mayes, Robert
Song of Our Savior	Perry, Julia
Song of Praise	Fax, Mark
Song of Praise, A	Hancock, Eugene
Song of the Liberty Bell	Price, John E.
Songs of Our Time	Logan, Wendell
Sonnet	Fax, Mark
Soon-a Will Be Done	Clark, Rogie
Soon A' Will Be Done	Williams, Julius, Jr.
Soon Ah Will Be Done (SATB)	Dawson, William L.
Soon Ah Will Be Done (TTBB)	Dawson, William L.
Soon I Will Be Done	Boatner, Edward
Soon I Will Be Done	Roberts, Howard
Sound Sleep by Night (from The Quiet Life)	Furman, James
Southern Lullaby	Burleigh, Harry T.
Spirituals	Anderson, T. J.
Spring (from Seasons)	Tillis, Frederick
Spring, The	Williams, Julius, Jr.
Stan' Still, Jordan	Johnson, J. Rosamond
Stand the Storm	Billups, Kenneth
Star, The	Boatner, Edward
Starry Night (from Two Dunbar Lyrics)	Kay, Ulysses
Stars	Walker, George
Steal Away	Burleigh, Harry T.
Steal Away	Carter, Roland

Talk About a Chile	Kerr, Thomas H., Jr.
Talking 'Bout Your Servant	Williams, Henry
Tall Tales	Adams, Leslie
Tambourines to Glory	Moore, Undine
Tataleo	Hairston, Jester
Te Deum	Cooper, William B.
Te Deum Laudamus	McLin, Lena
Tears	Childs, John
Tears, Flow No More	Kay, Ulysses
Tell Me, Shepherdess (from Christmas in the Western World)	Still, William Grant
That Old House Is Haunted	Hairston, Jester
That We May Live	Rivers, Clarence
That Yonge Child	Roxbury, Ronald
Them Dry Bones	Ryder, Noah
There Is a Balm in Gilead (SSA)	Dawson, William L.
There Is a Balm in Gilead (SATB)	Dawson, William L.
There Is a Balm in Gilead (TTBB)	Dawson, William L.
There Is No Rose of Such Virtue	Roxbury, Ronald
There Is None Like Him	Rivers, Clarence J.
There's a Lit'l Wheel a Turnin'	Dawson, William L.
There's a Man Goin' Round	Clark, Rogie
There's a Meeting Here Tonight	Dett, R. Nathaniel
There's a Meeting Here Tonight	Work, John W., III
There's a Star in the East	Hancock, Eugene
There's No Hiding Place	Gillum, Ruth H.
There's No Hiding Place Down There	Southall, Mitchell
They Crucified My Lord	Mells, Herbert F.
They Saw a Star	Mells, Herbert F.
They Shall Run and Not Be Weary	Taylor, Maude
They That Sow in Tears	Handy, W. C.
This House	Anderson, T. J.
This Is God's Place	Hancock, Eugene
This Land	McLin, Lena
This Little Light o' Mine	Work, John W., III
This Little Light of Mine	Fax, Mark
This Little Light of Mine	King, Betty Jackson
This Little Light of Mine	Moore, Dorothy R.
This Ol' Hammer	Ryder, Noah
This Ol' Hammer	Work, John W., III
This Old Hammer	White, Clarence C.

Ven Novo Divino (from Christmas in the Western World)	Still, William Grant
Victory Tide	Still, William Grant
Virgen Mary Had a Baby Boy, De (from Christmas in the Western World)	Still, William Grant
Voice of the Lord, The (Psalm XXIX)	Still, William Grant
Wade in de Water	Burleigh, Harry T.
Wade in de Water	Hairston, Jester
Wade in de Waters	Southall, Mitchell
Wade in the Water (SATB)	Clark, Rogie
Wade in the Water (SSA)	Clark, Rogie
Walk Through the Streets of the City	Moore, Undine
Walk Together Children	Burleigh, Harry T.
Walk Together Chillun	Johnson, Hall
Wasn't That a Mighty Day	Dett, R. Nathaniel
Wasn't That a Mighty Day (SATB)	Work, John W., III
Wasn't That a Mighty Day (SSA)	Work, John W., III
Waters of Life, The	Stor, Jean
'Way Over in Beulah Lan'	Johnson, Hall
'Way Over in Egypt Land	Work, John W., III
Way Up in Heaven	Johnson, Hall
We Are Climbing Jacob's Ladder	Da Costa, Noel
We Are the Men	Mells, Herbert F.
We Delighted, My Friend	Swanson, Howard
We Gonna Make It (from Two Prayers)	Cunningham, Arthur
We Shall Overcome	Fax, Mark
We Shall Walk Through the Valley	Moore, Undine
Weep You No More	Margetson, Edward
Weeping Mary	Dett, R. Nathaniel
Welcome Yule (from A Wreath for Waits)	Kay, Ulysses
We'll Go On and Serve the Lord	Handy, W. C.
We're Goin' to That Ball	Hairston, Jester
Were You There? (SATB)	Burleigh, Harry T.
Were You There? (SSA)	Burleigh, Harry T.
Were You There	Fax, Mark
Were You There	Johnson, Hall
Were You There (SATB)	Montague, J. Harold
Were You There (TTBB)	Montague, J. Harold
What Kind o' Shoes	Hariston, Jester
What Kinder Shoes	Hall, Johnson
What Month Was Jesus Born In?	Price, John E.
What Will You Put Under the Christmas Tree?	McLin, Lena

You Must Have That True Religion   Carter, Roland
You'd Better Run   Whalum, Wendell
You're Tired Chile   Duncan, John

Zion's Walls   Dawson, William L.

EDWARD BOATNER

SPIRITUALS TRIUMPHANT--OLD AND NEW

Edited and Arranged by Edward Boatner
Assisted by Mrs. Willa A. Townsend
Published by Sunday School Publishing Board
National Baptist Convention, U. S. A.
1927

1. Ain't You Glad
2. A Little Talk with Jesus
3. All O' My Sins
4. A New Hiding Place
5. Balm in Gilead
6. Blessed Are the Poor in Spirit
7. Build Right on That Shore
8. Can I Ride
9. Certainly Lord
10. Children Don't Get Weary
11. Couldn't Hear Nobody Pray
12. Crucifixion
13. Deep Down in My Heart
14. Deep River
15. Do, Lord, Remember Me
16. Done With Sin and Sorrow
17. Don't Let It Be Said Too Late
18. Down by the Riverside
19. Everytime I Feel the Spirit
20. Four and Twenty Elders
21. Get Right with God
22. Give Me Your Hand
23. Glory, Glory Hallelujah
24. Go Down Moses
25. God's Going to Set This World on Fire
26. Good News
27. Great Camp Meeting
28. Great Day
29. He Arose
30. He's Got His Eyes on Me
31. He's Got the Whole World in His Hands
32. How Did You Feel

33. Hush, Hush, Amen
34. I Am Bound for the Promised Land
35. I Can't Stay Away
36. I Don't Feel Noways Tired
37. I Know the Lord
38. I'm a Soldier
39. I'm in Your Care
40. I'm So Glad
41. In Bright Mansions Above
42. In My Father's House
43. In the River of Jordan
44. I Shall Not Be Moved
45. It's Me
46. I've Got a Robe
47. Jesus Is a Rock in a Weary Land
48. Let Me Ride
49. Let the Words
50. Listen to the Lambs
51. Look Away into Heaven
52. Lord, I Want to Be a Christian
53. Move Up the King's Highway
54. My Good Lord's Been Here
55. My Lord, What a Mourning
56. My Lord's Writing All the Time
57. No Hiding Place
58. Nobody Knows
59. None but the Righteous
60. Now Is the Needy Time
61. O Lord, Abide with Me
62. O My Lord, What Shall I Do
63. Oh, Freedom
64. Old Time Religion
65. On Calvary
66. Rise, Shine for Thy Light Is A-Coming
67. Room Enough
68. Shine for Jesus
69. Sit Down Servant
70. Somebody's Knocking at Your Door
71. Something Within
72. Steal Away
73. Sure He Died on Calvary
74. Swing Low, Sweet Chariot
75. The Church Is Moving On
76. The Time Ain't Long
77. There Is a Light Shining
78. There Is Joy in That Land
79. Wade in the Water
80. Walk With Me
81. We Shall Walk Through the Valley
82. Were You There?
83. When the Lord Shall Appear
84. When the Saints Go Marching In
85. Will the Lighthouse Shine on Me
86. Witness for My Lord
87. You Must Have That True Religion

EDWARD BOATNER

30 AFRO-AMERICAN CHORAL SPIRITUALS

Arranged by Edward Boatner
Published by Hammon Music Company
1964

General

Ain't That Good News
Done Made My Vow
City Called Heaven
See the Four and Twenty Elders
Hush, Hush
You Got to Reap
Hold On
My God Is So High
Oh, What a Beautiful City
Swing Low
I Know the Lord
On My Journey
I've Been 'Buked
Lost Sheep
Joshua
That Gettin' Up Morn'
Create Me a Body

He Is King of Kings
Let Us Break Bread Together
Don't Feel No Way Tired

Lenten

My Time Is Come
They Led My Lord Away
Calvary
He Arose
Were You There
Rise and Shine

Christmas

Behold That Star
Go Tell It on the Mountain
Rise Up Shepherds and Follow
New Born

CHARLES L. COOKE

ROBBINS CHORAL COLLECTION

Negro Spirituals for Mixed Voices
Arranged by Charles L. Cooke
Piano Accompaniment
Robbins Company
1942

1. Deep River
2. Give Me That Old Time Religion
3. Go Down Moses
4. Gospel Train
5. Heav'n, Heav'n
6. Joshua Fit de Battle of Jericho
7. Nobody Knows the Trouble I've Had
8. Sometimes I Feel Like a Motherless Child
9. Steal Away
10. Swing Low, Sweet Chariot
11. We Are Climbing Jacob's Ladder

R. NATHANIEL DETT

THE DETT COLLECTION OF NEGRO SPIRITUALS

FIRST GROUP, Originals, Settings, Anthems and Motets
Arranged by R. Nathaniel Dett
Schmitt, Hall-McCreary
1936

1. Balm in Gilead
2. Daniel Saw the Stone
3. Deep River

4. Don't Call the Roll, John
5. Give Me Your Hand
6. Go Down, Moses
7. Go, Tell It on the Mountain
8. I Hope My Mother Will Be There
9. I Know the Lord's Laid His Hands on Me
10. I've Done What You Told Me to Do
11. I Want to Be Ready
12. Keep Me from Sinking Down
13. Lord, I Want to Be a Christian
14. Many Thousand Gone
15. Mary and Martha
16. My Brother, I Do Wonder
17. My Way's Cloudy
18. Nobody Knows the Trouble I've Seen
19. O, I Got a Light
20. Poor Mourner's Got a Home
21. Rise and Shine
22. Room Enough
23. Shine Along
24. Somebody's Knocking at Your Door
25. Steal Away
26. Sweetest Sound I Ever Heard
27. Swing Low, Sweet Chariot
28. There's a Meeting Here Tonight

SECOND GROUP, Originals, Settings, Anthems and Motets with essay "Understanding the Negro Spiritual"
Arranged by R. Nathaniel Dett

1. Dust, Dust and Ashes
2. I Am Seeking for a City
3. Let the Heaven Light Shine on Me
4. Murm'ring Word
5. My Lord, What a Morning
6. Old Arks A-Movering Along, The
7. Save Me, Lord, Save Lord
8. Stay in the Field
9. 'Tis the Old Ship of Zion
10. We Are Building on a Rock
11. We Are Climbing Jacob's Ladder (Community setting)
12. We Are Climbing Jacob's Ladder (Choir setting)
13. What You Going t'Do When the Lamp Burns Down?
14. Winter'll Soon Be Over, The
15. You're Going to Reap Just What You Sow

THIRD GROUP, Originals, Settings, Anthems and Motets with essay "The Authenticity of the Spiritual"
Arranged by R. Nathaniel Dett

1. Appolyon and the Pilgrim
2. Better Be Ready
3. Calvary's Mountain
4. Certainly, Lord
5. Down in Hell
6. Father Abraham
7. I Ain't Going t'Study War No More
8. I Belong to the Union Band
9. In That Beautiful World on High

10. I've Got Shoes
11. Lord, Until I Reach My Home
12. Nobody Knows the Trouble I See, Lord
13. Poor Pilgrim
14. Roll, Jordan Roll (Circa 1860)
15. Roll, Jordan Roll (Tidewater Version)
16. Run to Jesus
17. Steal Away
18. We Are Trav'ling to the Grave

FOURTH GROUP, Originals, Settings, Anthems and Motets with essay "The Development of the
   Negro Spiritual"
Arranged by R. Nathaniel Dett

1. Baptism
2. By and By
3. Come to Me
4. Communion
5. Ev'ry Time I Feel the Spirit
6. Hew 'Round the Tree
7. Ho, Everyone That Thirsts
8. If I Had Died When I Was a Babe
9. Is There Anybody Here?
10. Little David, Play on Your Harp
11. O Holy Savior
12. On That Sabbath Morn
13. Pray on the Way
14. Roll, Jordan, Roll

R. NATHANIEL DETT

RELIGIOUS FOLK SONGS OF THE NEGRO AS SUNG AT HAMPTON INSTITUTE

Arranged and Edited by R. Nathaniel Dett
1927

1. A Wheel in a Wheel
2. Babylon's Fallin'
3. Band ob Gideon
4. Bright Sparkles in de Churchyard
5. But He Ain't Comin' Here t' Die No Mo'
6. By and By
7. Children, We Shall All Be Free
8. Come Down, Sinner
9. Daniel Saw the Stone
10. De Church of God
11. Deep River
12. De Ole Ark a-Moverin' Along
13. De Ole Sheep Done Know de Road
14. Dere's a Little Wheel a-Turnin' in My Heart
15. De Winter'll Soon Be Ober
16. Did You Hear How Dey Crucified My Lord?
17. Don't Be Weary, Traveller
18. Don't Call de Roll
19. Don't Get Weary
20. Don't Leave Me Lord
21. Don't You View Dat Ship A-Come A-Sailin'

22. Down By the River
23. Dust an' Ashes
24. Ef You Want to Get to Hebben
25. Ev'ry Time I Feel the Spirit
26. Ezekiel Saw de Wheel
27. Fighting On
28. Git on Board, Little Children
29. Go Down, Moses
30. Going to Heaven
31. Goin' to Shout All over God's Heav'n
32. Go, Mary, an' Toll de Bell
33. Good Lord, Shall I Ever Be de One?
34. Good News, de Chariot's Comin'
35. Go Tell It on de Mountain
36. Grace Before Meal at Hampton
37. Gwine to Live Humble to de Lord
38. Gwine Up
39. Hail, Hail, Hail
40. Hard Trials
41. Hear de Angels Singin'
42. Hear de Lambs A-Cryin'
43. He Is King of Kings
44. He's the Lily of the Valley
45. I Ain't Goint' Study War No More
46. I Am Goin' to Join in This Army
47. I Am Seekin' for a City
48. I Couldn't Hear Nobody Pray
49. I Don't Want to Stay Here No Longer
50. If You Love God, Serve Him
51. I Heard from Heaven To-Day
52. I Heard the Preaching of the Elder
53. I Know the Lord's Laid His Hands on Me
54. I'll Be There in the Morning
55. I'm A-Rolling
56. I'm A-Trav'ling to the Grave
57. I'm Gwine to Jine de Great 'Sociation
58. I'm So Glad Trouble Don't Last Alway
59. I'm Troubled in Mind
60. In Bright Mansions Above
61. In Dat Great Gettin'-Up Mornin'
62. In That Beautiful World on High
63. In the Kingdom
64. I've Been A-List'ning All de Night Long
65. I've Been Toilin' at de Hill
66. I've Got a Mother in de Heaven
67. I Want to be Ready
68. I Would Like to Read
69. Jerusalem Mornin'
70. John Saw
71. Judgement
72. Keep A-Inchin' Along
73. Keep Me from Sinkin' Down
74. King Emanuel
75. Leanin' on de Lord
76. L'Envoi
77. Let de Heaven Light Shine on Me
78. Let Us Cheer the Weary Traveler
79. Let Us Praise Him
80. Like a Rough and a Rolling Sea
81. Listen to de Lambs
82. Little David, Play on Your Harp

83. Live Humble
84. Look Away
85. Lord, Have Mercy
86. Lord, I Want to Be a Christian
87. Lord, Until I Reach My Home
88. Most Done Travelling
89. Mother, Is Massa Gwine to Sell Us?
90. My Lord Delibered Daniel
91. My Lord's A-Riding All the Time
92. My Lord, What a Morning
93. My Soul Wants Something That's New
94. My Way's Cloudy
95. Nobody Knows de Trouble I've Seen
96. No More Auction Block
97. Oh, de Downward Road Is Crowded
98. Oh, de Hebben Is Shinin'
99. Oh, Freedom
100. Oh, Give Way, Jordan
101. Oh, He Raise-a Poor Lazarus
102. Oh, Jerusalem
103. Oh, Religion Is a Fortune
104. Oh, Sinner, You'd Better Get Ready
105. Oh, Stand the Storm
106. Oh, the Rocks and the Mountains
107. Oh, Wasn't Dat a Wide Riber
108. Oh, When I Get t' Heaven
109. Oh, Yes
110. Oh, Yes, Yonder Comes My Lord
111. Ole-Time Religion
112. Peter on the Sea
113. Pilgrim's Song
114. Poor Pilgrim
115. Prayer Is de Key of Heaven
116. Put John on de Islan'
117. 'Raslin' Jacob
118. Reign, Massa Jesus
119. Ride On
120. Ride On, Jesus
121. Rise an' Shine
122. Rise Up, Shepherd, an' Foller
123. Roll de Ole Chariot Along
124. Roll, Jordan, Roll
125. Run, Mary, Run
126. Run to Jesus
127. See Fo' and Twenty Elders
128. Seek and Ye Shall Find
129. Slav'ry Chain
130. Somebody's Knocking at Your Door
131. Sometimes I Feel Like a Motherless Child
132. Soon I Will Be Done
133. Stars in the Elements
134. Stay in de Field
135. Steal Away to Jesus
136. Sun Don't Set In de Mornin'
137. Sweet Canaan
138. Sweet Turtle Dove
139. Swing Low, Chariot
140. Swing Low, Sweet Chariot
141. Swing Low, Sweet Chariot (App. V)
142. Tell Jesus
143. There Is a Balm in Gilead

144. There's a Meeting Here To-Night
145. There Were Ten Virgins
146. They Look Like Men of War
147. 'Tis Me
148. 'Tis the Ole Ship of Zion
149. View de Land
150. Walk Togedder, Children
151. Walk You in de Light
152. Want to Go to Heaven When I Die
153. We Are Almost Home
154. We Are Building on a Rock
155. We Are Climbing Jacob's Ladder
156. We Are Walking in de Light
157. Were You There When They Crucified My Lord?
158. What You' Gwine t' Do When de Lamp Burn Down?
159. When the General Roll Is Called
160. Where Shall I Be When de Firs' Trumpet Soun'?
161. Who'll Jine de Union
162. Why, He's the Lord of Lords
163. Wonder Where Is Good Ole Daniel
164. You Goin' to Reap Jus' What You Sow
165. Zion, Weep a-Low

CARL DITON

THIRTY-SIX SOUTH CAROLINA SPIRITUALS

Set 12
Collected and Harmonized by Carl Diton
Schirmer's American Folk-Song Series
1930

1. I Want to Climb Up Jacob's Ladder
2. When the Train Comes Along
3. I Wish I Have Had an Eagle Wing
4. Holy, Holy, You Promised to Answer Prayer
5. Ev'ry Time I Feel the Spirit
6. Jesus Rides That Milk-White Horse
7. I Ain' Gwine to Grieve My Lord No More
8. I've Got a Home in the Rock, Don't You See
9. The Blood Done Signed My Name
10. I'm A-Going to Eat at the Welcome Table
11. Way in the Heaven Bye and Bye
12. Going to Pull Any War-Clothes
13. Never Leave Me Alone
14. Motherless Children Have a Hard Time
15. May Be the Last Time, I Don't Know
16. All I Do, the People Keep A-Grumbeling
17. Band of Angels
18. Road Is Rugged, But I Must Go
19. This Is the Man
20. Fisherman Peter
21. Stand on the Sea of Glass
22. Funeral Chant
23. Weep No More for Baby
24. Ring the Bells
25. When You Hear My Coffin Sound
26. Ezekiel Said There Was a Wheel in a Wheel
27. Ride On, Conquering King

28. Fix Me, Jesus
29. You Go, I'll Go with You
30. Every Little Step Goes Higher
31. I've Been Trying to Live Humble
32. I Can't Stay Behind
33. Walk In Jerusalem, Just Like John
34. Roll, Jordan, Roll
35. Same Train
36. Look Away in the Heaven

FISK UNIVERSITY

JUBILEE SONGS

As sung by the Jubilee Singers of Fisk University
1872

1. Been A-Listening
2. Children, We Shall All Be Free
3. Children, You'll Be Called On
4. Didn't My Lord Deliver Daniel
5. From Every Graveyard
6. Give Me Jesus
7. Gwine to Ride Up the Chariot
8. Go Down Moses
9. I'm A-Rolling
10. I'll Hear the Trumpet Sound
11. I've Just Come from the Fountain
12. I'm a Traveling to the Grave
13. Keep Me from Sinking Down
14. Many Thousand Gone
15. Nobody Knows the Trouble I See, Lord
16. O Redeemed
17. Room Enough
18. Roll Jordan Roll
19. Rise, Mourners Rise
20. Swing Low
21. Steal Away
22. Turn Back Pharoah's Army
23. The Rocks and the Mountains
24. We'll Die in the Field

JESTER HAIRSTON and HARRY ROBERT WILSON

NEGRO SPIRITUALS AND FOLK SONGS

For Mixed Voices
Selected and Arranged by Jester Hairston and Harry Robert Wilson
Published by Bourne Company
Background material on the history and interpretation of Negro Folk Music; complete program
notes for each song
1960

1. Angels Rolled de Stone Away
2. Aurore Pradere

3.   Brother Rabbit
4.   Free At Last
5.   Give Me Jesus
6.   I Heard from Heaven Today
7.   My Lord's A-Writin' All de Time
8.   Nobody Knows de Trouble I See, Lord
9.   Oh My Lovin' Brother
10.   Po' Ol' Lazrus
11.   Sandy Anna (TTBB)
12.   Sanguree
13.   Somebody's Knocking at Your Door
14.   Sweet Potatoes
15.   Wasn't That a Mighty Day?
16.   You Better Mind

FREDERICK DOUGLASS HALL

NEGRO SPIRITUALS

For Mixed Voices
Arranged by Frederick Hall
Published by Rodeheaver, Hall-Mack Company
1939

1.   City Called Heaven
2.   Crucifixion
3.   Day Is Done
4.   Go Down Moses
5.   Golden Slippers
6.   Home in Dat Rock
7.   Jacob's Ladder
8.   Live a-Humble
9.   Mos' Done Toilin'
10.   My Way Is Cloudy
11.   Nobody Knows de Trouble I See
12.   Two Wings

NEGRO SPIRITUALS

For Women's Voices
Arranged by Frederick Hall
Published by Rodeheaver, Hall-Mack Company
1939

1.   Deep River
2.   I Stood on de River of Jordan
3.   Keep a'Inchin' Along
4.   Ol' Time Religion
5.   Set Down
6.   Somebody's Knowckin' at Yo' Do'
7.   Talk About a Chile dat Do Love Jesus
8.   Were You There
9.   Wade in de Water
10.   You Got to Reap What You Sow

NEGRO SPIRITUALS AND FOLK SONGS

For Men's Voices
Arranged by Frederick Hall
Published by Rodeheaver, Hall-Mack Company
1939

1. Ain't It a Shame
2. Balm in Gilead
3. Bye an' Bye
4. Cert'nly Lord
5. Climbin' up de Mountain
6. Dry Bones
7. Joshua Fit de Battle
8. Mam's Li'l Boy
9. O Mary
10. Old Black Joe
11. Po Li'l Lam'

FREDERICK HALL

SONGS OF THE SOUTHLAND

Arranged by Frederick Hall
1955

Number I, TTBB

1. Holy unto the Lord
2. Inchin' Along
3. Let Us Break Bread
4. Li'l David
5. My Lord's Gonna Move
6. Nobody Knows
7. Scandalizin' My Name
8. The Crucifixion

Number II, SSA

1. Climbin' Up de Mountain
2. Git'n Up Mornin'
3. Go Down Moses
4. Good News
5. Li'l Wheel
6. 'Zekiel Saw de Wheel

Number III, SATB

1. Ain't Dat Good News
2. Great Day
3. Hallelujah
4. I Can Tell the World
5. I Want to Be Ready
6. Live a-Humble
7. New Born
8. Rise-Shine

9.   Somebody's Knockin' at Yo' Do'
10.   Stan' de Storm
11.   Trampin'
12.   Wait 'Till I Put on My Crown

EUGENE W. HANCOCK

THIRTEEN SPIRITUALS

For Equal Voices in Unison and Two Parts
Organ and Unaccompanied
Arranged by Eugene W. Hancock
Published by H. W. Gray
1973

1.   Calvary
2.   Go, Tell It on the Mountain
3.   I'm Troubled in Mind
4.   Let Us Break Bread Together
5.   Lord, I Want to Be a Christian
6.   My Soul's Been Anchored in the Lord
7.   O Redeemed
8.   Swing Low, Sweet Chariot
9.   There's a Star in the East
10.   Wade in the Water
11.   Walk Together, Children
12.   Were You There

WILLIAM C. HANDY

SECOND COLLECTION OF 37 SPIRITUALS

Mixed Voices, Male Voices and Vocal Solos with Piano Accompaniment
Arranged by William C. Handy
Published by Handy Brothers Music Company
1938

1.   I've Heard of a City Called Heaven (SATB)
2.   I've Been in de Storm So Long (SATB)
3.   Shine Like a Morning Star (SATB)
4.   Children, You'll Be Called On (SATB)
5.   You Better Mind (SATB)
6.   Get Right, Church, Get Right (SATB)
7.   I'll Be There in the Morning (SATB)
8.   I'm Drinking from a Fountain (SATB)
9.   See the Sign of the Judgement (SATB)
10.   Rise, Shine, For Thy Light Is A-Coming (SATB)
11.   Keep Me from Sinking Down (SATB)
12.   One Found Worthy (SATB)
13.   Jesus Goin' a Make Up My Dying Bed (SATB)
14.   Stand on the Rock a Little Longer (SATB)
15.   We'll Go On and Serve the Lord (SATB)
16.   Turn Back Pharaoh's Army, Hallelu (SATB)
17.   Judgement Day Is Rolling Around (SATB)
18.   Give Me Jesus (SATB)

19. Let Us Cheer the Weary Traveller (SATB)
20. Stand on That Sea of Glass (SATB)
21. The Bridegroom Has Done Come (SATB)
22. 'Tis the Old Ship of Zion (SATB)
23. Steal Away to Jesus (SATB)
24. Hist de Window Noah (SATB)
25. Swing Low, Sweet Chariot (SATB)
26. Nobody Knows de Trouble I See, Lord (Solo)
27. The Rough Rocky Road (Solo)
28. I'll Never Turn Back (Solo)
29. I Want to Be Ready (TTBB)
30. The Gospel Train (TTBB)
31. Sunday Morning Band (TTBB)
32. Room Enough (TTBB)
33. The Rocks and the Mountains (TTBB)
34. I've Just Come from the Fountain (TTBB)
35. My Lord's Writing All the Time (TTBB)
36. Been A Listening (TTBB)
37. Somebody's Wrong About Dis Bible (SATB/Solo)

HAMPTON INSTITUTE

CABIN AND PLANTATION SONGS
As sung by the Hampton Students
Arranged by Thomas P. Fenner, Frederic G. Rathbun, and Miss Bessie Cleaveland, musical
   instructors in the Hampton Normal and Agricultural Institute of Virginia
1901
(Reprint of the 1901 ed. published by AMS Press)

1. A Great Camp-meetin' in de Promised Land
2. A Wheel in a Wheel
3. Babylon's Fallin'
4. Bright Sparkles in the Churchyard
5. Come Down, Sinner
6. De Church ob God
7. De Ole Ark A-Moverin'
8. De Ole Sheep Done Know de Road
9. Dere's a Little Wheel A-Turnin'
10. De Winter'll Soon Be Ober
11. Did You Hear How Dey Crucified My Lord?
12. Did You Hear My Jesus
13. Don't Be Weary Traveller
14. Don't Call de Roll
15. Don't Leave Me Lord
16. Don't Ye View Dat Ship A-Come A-Sailin'?
17. Dust an' Ashes
18. Ef You Want to See Jesus
19. Fighting On
20. General Roll Call
21. Gideon's Band, or de Milk-White Horses
22. Git on Board, Little Children
23. Glory and Honor
24. Going to Heaven
25. Go, Mary, an' Toll de Bell
26. Good Lord, Shall I Ever Be de One?
27. Good News, de Chariot's Comin'
28. Grace Before Meal at Hampton
29. Gwin to Live Humble to de Lord

30. Gwin Up
31. Hail, Hail, Hail
32. Hard Trials
33. Hear de Angels Singin'
34. Hear de Lambs a-Crying
35. He Is King of Kings
36. He Raise a Poor Lazarus
37. He's the Lord of Lords
38. I Don't Feel No-ways Tired
39. I Hope My Mother Will Be There
40. I Know I Would Like to Read
41. I'll Be There in the Morning
42. I'm A-Rolling Through an Unfriendly World
43. I'm A-Trav'ling to the Grave
44. I'm Goin' to Join in This Army
45. In Bright Mansions Above
46. In Dat Great Gittin'-Up Mornin'
47. In the Kingdom
48. I've Been A-List'nin' All de Night Long
49. I've Been Toilin' at de Hill
50. I've Got a Mother in de Heaven
51. Jacob's Ladder
52. Jesus Ain't Comin' Here t' Die No Mo'
53. John Saw
54. Judgement-Day Is A-Rollin' Around
55. Keep Me from Sinkin' Down
56. King Emanuel
57. Let de Heaven Light Shine on Me
58. Let Us Praise Him
59. Little David, Play on Your Harp
60. Love an' Serve de Lord
61. Many Thousands Gone
62. Massa Gwine to Sell Us To-morrow
63. Most Done Trabelin'
64. My Brethern, Don't Get Weary
65. My Lord Delibered Daniel
66. My Lord's A-Riding All the Time
67. My Lord, What a Mornin'
68. My Soul Wants Something That's New
69. My Way's Cloudy
70. Nobody Knows de Trouble I've Seen
71. Oh, de Hebben Is Shinin'
72. Oh, Den My Little Soul's Gwine to Shine
73. Oh, Freedom
74. Oh, Give Way Jordan
75. Oh, Jerusalem
76. Oh, Sinner, You'd Better Get Ready
77. Oh, Wasn't Dat a Wide Riber?
78. Oh, When I Git t'Heaven
79. Oh, Yes
80. Oh, Yes, Yonder Comes My Lord
81. Ole Ship of Zion
82. Peter, Go Ring dem Bells
83. Peter on the Sea
84. Pilgrim's Song
85. Prayer Is de Key of Heaven
86. Put John on de Island
87. Raslin' Jacob
88. Religion Is a Fortune
89. Ride On
90. Rise an' Shine

91.   Roll de Ole Chariot Along
92.   Rough and Rolling Sea
93.   Run, Mary, Run
94.   See Fo' an' Twenty Elders
95.   Seek and Ye Shall Find
96.   Some o' Dese Mornin's
97.   Sometimes I Feel Like a Motherless Child
98.   Stars in the Elements Are Falling
99.   Stay in the Field
100.   Sun Don't Set in de Mornin'
101.   Sweet Canaan
102.   Sweet Turtle Dove, or Jerusalem Mornin'
103.   Swing Low, Chariot
104.   Swing Low, Sweet Chariot
105.   Tell Jesus
106.   The Danville Chariot
107.   The Downward Road Is Crowded
108.   The Enlisted Soldiers
109.   There Were Ten Virgins
110.   View de Land
111.   Walking in the Light
112.   Walk You in de Light
113.   We Are Building on a Rock
114.   What Yo' Gwine t' Do When de Lamp Burn Down?
115.   When I Come to Die
116.   Who'll Jine de Union?
117.   Wonder Where Is Good Ole Daniel
118.   Zion, Weep a-Low

Indian

119.   Love Song, Sioux
120.   Night Dance, Sioux
121.   War Song, Sioux

Japanese

122.   Tencho-Setsu no Uta

Hawaiian

123.   Aloha oe
124.   Hawaii Ponoi

Chinese

125.   The Lily Song

126.   Turkish Song

HAMPTON INSTITUTE

RELIGIOUS FOLK SONGS OF THE NEGRO

Arranged by the Musical Directors of the Hampton Normal and Agricultural Institute
1920
(Reprint, AMS Press)

(In this edition 26 new arrangements were added to Cabin and Plantation Songs.   Only the new
   additions are listed.)

1. Daniel Saw de Stone
2. Down by de River
3. Ev'ry Time I Feel de Spirit
4. Ezekiel Saw de Wheel
5. Go Down, Moses
6. Going to Shout All over God's Heav'n
7. Go Tell It on the Mountain
8. I Couldn't Hear Nobody Pray
9. I Know de Lord's Laid His Hands on Me
10. I Want to Be Ready
11. Keep A-Inchin' Along
12. Let Us Cheer the Weary Traveller
13. Listen to the Lambs
14. Little Wheel A-Turnin' in My Heart
15. Lord, I Want to Be a Christian
16. Lord, Until I Reach My Home
17. Reign, Massa Jesus
18. Rise Up Shepherd an' Foller
19. Roll, Jordan Roll
20. Somebody's Knocking at Your Door
21. Steal Away to Jesus
22. The Rocks and the Mountains
23. 'Tis Me, 'Tis Me, O Lord
24. Want to Go to Heaven When I Die
25. Were You There
26. Where Shall I Be When de Firs' Trumpet Soun'?

J. ROSAMOND JOHNSON

UTICA JUBILEE SINGERS SPIRITUALS

As sung at the Utica Normal and Industrial Institute of Mississippi
Taken down by J. Rosamond Johnson

1. All God's Chillun Got Wings
2. Angels Watchin' Over Me
3. De Ol' Ark's A-Moverin' an' I'm Goin' Home
4. Don't You Want to Be a Lover of the Lord
5. Down By de Riverside
6. Do You Call Dat Religion
7. Ezekiel
8. Good News, Chariot Comin'
9. Go Tell It on de Mountain
10. Hand Me Down
11. Humble Yo' Self
12. Hush, Hush
13. I Couldn't Hear Nobody Pray
14. I Know de Lord Has Laid His Han's on Me
15. I'm Goin' to Meet My Mother
16. I'm Troubled, Lord
17. It's Me, O Lord

18. Jubalee
19. Keep A-Inchin' Along
20. King Jesus Is A-Lis'enin'
21. My Lord's Goin' to Move Dis Wicked Race
22. Little David
23. Lord, I Done What You Tol' Me to Do
24. Nobody Knows de Trouble I See
25. Now Let Me Fly
26. O Mary Don't You Weep
27. O My Good Lord
28. O Wasn't That a Mighty Day
29. Peter on the Sea
30. Rise, Shine
31. Run to My Lord
32. Steal Away to Jesus
33. Swing Low Sweet Chariot
34. Walk in Jerusalem Jus' Like John
35. Where Shall I Go
36. Witness for My Lord
37. Leanin' on de Lord
38. You Bettah Mind

J. B. T. MARSH

THE STORY OF THE JUBILEE SINGERS, With Their Songs

Originally published in 1881, Houghton, Mifflin and Co., Boston
Reprinted 1969, Negro Universities Press
(Chapters I-XI: Story of the Jubilee Singers)

Index to Music

1. A Happy New Year
2. A Little More Faith in Jesus
3. Anchor in the Lord
4. Angels Waiting at the Door
5. Been a Listening
6. Bright Sparkles in the Churchyard
7. Children, You'll Be Called On
8. Children, We All Shall Be Free
9. Come Down Angels
10. Come, Let Us All Go Down
11. Deep River
12. Did Not Old Pharaoh Get Lost?
13. Didn't My Lord Deliver Daniel
14. Don't You Grieve After Me
15. Down by the River
16. Farewell, My Brother
17. From Every Graveyard
18. Gabriel's Trumpet's Going to Blow
19. Getting Ready to Die
20. Gideon's Band
21. Give Me Jesus
22. Go Down Moses
23. Go, Chain the Lion Down
24. Good-bye, Brothers
25. Good Old Chariot

26.   Grace
27.   Gwine to Ride Up in the Chariot
28.   Hard Trials
29.   He Arose
30.   He Rose from the Dead
31.   He's the Lily of the Valley
32.   He's the Lord of Lords
33.   I Am Going to Die No More
34.   I Ain't Got Weary Yet
35.   I Know That My Redeemer Lives
36.   I'll Hear the Trumpet Sound
37.   I'm a Rolling
38.   I'm a Travelling to the Grave
39.   I'm Going to Live with Jesus
40.   I'm So Glad
41.   I'm Troubled in Mind
42.   In Bright Mansions Above
43.   Inching Along
44.   In the River of Jordan
45.   In That Great Getting-Up Morning
46.   I've Been Redeemed
47.   I've Just Come from the Fountain
48.   John Brown's Body
49.   Judgement-Day Is Rolling Round
50.   Judgement Will Find You So
51.   Keep Me From Sinking Down
52.   Keep Your Lamps Trimmed and Burning
53.   Listen to the Angels
54.   Love Feast in Heaven
55.   Lord, I Wish I Had Come
56.   Lord's Prayer
57.   Many Thousand Gone
58.   March On
59.   Mary and Martha
60.   Move Along
61.   My Good Lord's Been Here
62.   My Lord, What a Mourning
63.   My Ship Is on the Ocean
64.   My Way's Cloudy
65.   Nobody Knows the Trouble I See
66.   Now We Take This Feeble Body
67.   Oh! Holy Lord
68.   Oh, Wasn't That a Wide River
69.   Oh Yes, Oh Yes
70.   Old Ship of Zion
71.   O, Let Me Get Up
72.   O, Redeemed
73.   O Sinner Man
74.   Peter, Go Ring Them Bells
75.   Prepare Us
76.   Reign, O Reign
77.   Ride On, King Jesus
78.   Rise and Shine
79.   Rise, Mourners
80.   Roll, Jordan Roll
81.   Room Enough
82.   Run to Jesus
83.   Save Me, Lord, Save Me
84.   Shine, Shine
85.   Sweet Canaan
86.   Show Me the Way

87. Steal Away
88. Swing Low, Sweet Chariot
89. 'Tis Jordan's River
90. The General Roll
91. The Gospel Train
92. The Rocks and the Mountains
93. The Angels Changed My Name
94. These Are My Father's Children
95. There's a Meeting Here To-Night
96. The Ten Virgins
97. This Old Time Religion
98. Turn Back Pharaoh's Army
99. Wait a Little While
100. Way Over Jordan
101. We Are Almost Home
102. We Are Climbing the Hills of Zion
103. We'll Die in the Field
104. We'll Overtake the Army
105. We'll Stand the Storm
106. We Shall Walk Through the Valley
107. When Moses Smote the Water
108. When Shall I Get There
109. Wrestling Jacob
110. Zion's Children

CLARENCE CAMERON WHITE

TRADITIONAL NEGRO SPIRITUALS

SATB
Arranged by Clarence Cameron White

1. Can I Ride
2. Cert'nly, Lord
3. Down by the Riverside
4. Everytime I Feel the Spirit
5. Get on Board, Little Children
6. Hear the Good News
7. I Got a Robe
8. I Heard of a City Called Heaven
9. In That Great Gettin' Up Morning
10. I Want Jesus to Walk With Me
11. Look Away
12. Lonesome Valley
13. Lord, Hear Me Prayin'
14. Old-Time Religion
15. Ride On Jesus
16. Steal Away
17. Trouble Will Bury Me Down
18. Walk Together Children
19. We Are Climbing Jacob's Ladder
20. Were You There

FREDERICK J. WORK

NEW JUBILEE SONGS

As sung by the Fisk Jubilee Singers of Fisk University
Collected and Harmonized by Frederick J. Work
Fisk University, Nashville, Tennessee
1902

1.   A Little Talk with Jesus
2.   Ain't I Glad I've Got Out the Wilderness
3.   Before This Time Another Year
4.   By and By
5.   Can't You Live Humble?
6.   Christians, Hold Up Your Heads
7.   Give Me Jesus
8.   Going to Hold Out to the End
9.   Good Morning
10. Hallelujah
11. Holy Bible
12. I Am So Glad
13. I Have Another Building
14. I Heard the Praying of the Elders
15. I Know the Lord's Laid His Hands on Me
16. I'm A-Going to Join the Band
17. I'm A-Going to Lay Down My Life
18. I Wish I Had Died in Egypt Land
19. I Won't Stop Praying
20. Jesus Is Risen from the Dead
21. Let Us Cheer the Weary Traveller
22. Little David
23. Live a-Humble
24. Lord I Want to Be a Christian
25. My Good Lord's Done Been Here
26. My Name's Written on High
27. My Soul's Been Anchored in the Lord
28. O Mother, Don't You Weep
29. O' Nobody Knows Who I Am
30. O Rocks, Don't Fall on Me
31. Plenty Good Room
32. Religion Is a Fortune
33. Roll On
34. Show Me the Way
35. Sing a Ho That I Had Wings of a Dove
36. Sinner Please Don't Let This Harvest Pass
37. Somebody's Buried in the Graveyard
38. Steal Away to Jesus
39. Swing Low
40. Tell All the World, John
41. The Old Ark's A-Movering
42. This Is a Sin-Trying World
43. Wade in the Water
44. Want to Go to Heaven When I Die
45. Were You There?
46. When I'm Dead
47. You Won't Find a Man Like Jesus

JOHN W. WORK III

AMERICAN NEGRO SONGS AND SPIRITUALS

A comprehensive Collection of Folk Songs, Religious and Secular

Compiled by John W. Work III
Foreword by John W. Work III

1. Ain't I Glad I've Got Out of the Wilderness
2. Ain't That Good News?
3. Ain't You Glad You Got Good Religion
4. All Over This World
5. Angels Done Bowed Down
6. At the Bar of God
7. Balm in Gilead
8. Before This Time Another Year
9. Bet on Stuball
10. Be with Me
11. Bye and Bye (1)
12. Bye and Bye (2)
13. Calvary
14. Can't You Live Humble
15. Captain, O Captain
16. Captain Says Hurry
17. Come Down
18. Come Here Lord
19. Convict Song
20. Daniel Saw the Stone
21. Death Ain't Nothin' but a Robber
22. Death's Goin' to Lay His Hand on Me
23. Do Lord Remember Me
24. Done Made My Vow to the Lord
25. Don't You Let Nobody Turn You Roun'
26. Down on Me
27. Downward Road Is Crowded
28. Ev'ry Day'll Be Sunday
29. Ezek'el Saw the Wheel
30. Free at Last
31. Gift of God
32. Give Me Jesus
33. Give Me Your Hand
34. Glory to That Newborn King
35. God Is a God
36. Go Down 'n the Valley and Pray
37. Go Down Moses
38. God's Goin' to Straighten Them
39. Going Home in the Chariot
40. Going to Shout All Over God's Heav'n
41. Goin' to Keep My Skillet Greasy
42. Gonna Leave Big Rock Behind
43. Good Lord I Done Done
44. Good Morning Everybody
45. God a Home in That Rock
46. Go Tell It on the Mountain
47. Got My Letter
48. Got No Money
49. Got Religion All Around the World
50. Got to Go to Judgement
51. Great Day
52. Had to Get Up This Mornin'
53. Hallelu
54. Hallelujah
55. Hammering
56. Hammers Keep Ringing
57. Hear Me Praying
58. He Is King of Kings

59. He Never Said a Mumblin' Word
60. He's a Mighty Good Leader
61. He's Got His Eyes on You
62. Hold the Wind
63. Holy Bible
64. Hot Boilin' Sun Comin' Over
65. I Am the True Vine
66. I Believe This Is Jesus
67. I Couldn't Hear Nobody Pray
68. I Feel Like My Time Ain't Long
69. I Got a House in Baltimo'
70. I Have Another Building
71. I Heard the Preaching of the Elder
72. I Know the Lord's Laid His Hands on Me
73. I'll Be There
74. I'm A-Going to Do All I Can
75. I'm Agoing to Join the Band
76. I'm Going Back With Jesus
77. I'm Goin' to Sing
78. I'm Just a-Goin' Over There
79. I'm So Glad
80. I'm Working on the Buildin'
81. I Must Walk My Lonesome Valley
82. Inching Along
83. I Never Felt Such Love in My Soul Befo'
84. In This Lan'
85. Is There Anybody Here?
86. It's Me
87. I've Done What You Told Me to Do
88. I've Just Come from the Fountain
89. I Want to Be Ready
90. I Went Down in the Valley
91. I Will Pray
92. I Wish I Had Died in Egypt Land
93. I Won't Stop Praying
94. Jesus Is Risen from the Dead
95. Jesus Goin' to Make Up My Dying Bed
96. Jim Atrange Killed Lula
97. John Henry (1)
98. John Henry (2)
99. Jubilee
100. King Jesus Built Me a House Above
101. Lay Ten Dollars Down
102. Lead Me to the Rock
103. Let the Church Roll On
104. Let Us Cheer the Weary Traveller
105. Listen to the Angel's Shoutin'
106. Listen to the Lambs
107. Little David
108. Little Talk With Jesus
109. Live a Humble
110. Lord Is My Shepherd
111. Lord I Want to Be a Christian
112. Lord Make Me More Holy
113. Lord's Been Here
114. Lullaby
115. Mamma Dinah
116. Marching Up the Heavenly Road
117. March On
118. My Good Lord's Done Been Here
119. My Lord's Goin' Move This Wicked Race

120. My Lord What a Mourning
121. My Name's Written on High
122. My Sin's Been Taken Away
123. My Soul's Been Anchored in the Lord
124. Naw I Don't
125. New Born Again
126. Nobody Knows Who I Am
127. No Hiding Place
128. O It's Goin' to Be a Mighty Day
129. O Lamb, Beautiful Lamb
130. Old Ark's a Movering
131. Old Zion's Children Marchin' Along
132. Ol' Elder Brown's
133. O Lord I'm Hungry
134. O Make Me Holy
135. O Mary Don't You Weep Don't You Mourn
136. O Mother Don't You Weep
137. O My Little Soul
138. Open the Window Noah
139. O Rocks Don't Fall on Me
140. O Wretched Man
141. Plenty Good Room
142. Po' Ol' Laz'rus
143. Poor Me
144. Poor Mourner's Got a Home
145. Poor Sinner
146. Pray On
147. Railroad Bill
148. Religion Is a Fortune
149. Religion That My Lord Gave Me
150. Ride On King Jesus
151. Rise, Shine, For Thy Light Is A-Comin'
152. Road Gang Song
153. Rockin' Jerusalem
154. Rock of Ages
155. Rocks and the Mountains
156. Roll, Jordan, Roll
157. Roll On
158. Run, Mourner, Run
159. Screw This Cotton
160. Seben Times
161. See the Signs of Judgement
162. Shepherd, Shepherd
163. Shout for Joy
164. Show Me the Way
165. Sing a Ho That I Had the Wings of a Dove
166. Sinner Please Don't Let This Harvest Pass
167. Sit Down Servant, Sit Down
168. Sittin' Down Beside O' the Lamb
169. Somebody's Buried in the Graveyard
170. Somebody's Knocking at Your Door
171. Some of These Days
172. Sometimes I Feel Like a Motherless Chile
173. Soon A Will Be Done
174. Stand the Storm
175. Steady, Jesus Listenin'
176. Steal Away and Pray
177. Steal Away to Jesus
178. Street Song
179. Study War No More
180. Sunday Mornin' Ban

181. Sun Mows Down
182. Swing Low
183. Tell All the World, John
184. Thank God I'm on My Way to Heaven
185. There's a Great Camp Meeting
186. There's a Meeting Here Tonight
187. There's Room Enough
188. There's Something on My Mind
189. They Led My Lord Away
190. This Is a Sin-Trying World
191. This Ol' Time Religion
192. Tryin' to Cross the Red Sea
193. Tryin' to Get Home
194. 'Twas on One Sunday Morning
195. Vendor's Call
196. Wake Me
197. Want to Go to Heaven When I Die
198. Wasn't That a Mighty Day
199. We Are Climbing Jacob's Ladder
200. Were You There?
201. We Shall Walk Through the Valley
202. What Shall I Do?
203. When I'm Dead
204. When the Train Comes Along
205. Where Shall I Go?
206. Wish I's in Heaven Settin' Down
207. Witness
208. Workin' on the Railroad Line
209. Yo' Low Down Ways
210. You'd Better Min'
211. You'd Better Run
212. You Hear the Lambs A-Crying
213. You May Bury Me in the East
214. You're My Brother, So Give Me Your Han'

JOHN W. WORK III

JUBILEE: A COLLECTION OF 10 NEGRO SPIRITUALS

SATB, A Cappella
Compiled by John W. Work III
Published by Holt, Rinehart and Winston
1962

1. Were You There When They Crucified My Lord?
2. Keep Me from Sinking Down
3. Walk Together, Children
4. Oh Peter, Go Ring Dem Bells
5. Let Us Cheer the Weary Traveller
6. Run, Mourner, Run
7. Let Us Break Bread Together on Our Knees
8. We'll Die in the Field
9. Tell All the World, John
10. Go Down, Moses

BIOGRAPHICAL SKETCHES

_____

ADAMS, LESLIE. Composer, educator. Native of Cleveland. B. M. , Oberlin Conservatory; M. Mus.
(composition), California State University (Long Beach); doctorate, Ohio State University.
Held positions as Music Director of the New Mexico School for Performing Arts and Associate Professor and Administrative Associate, University of Kansas. Presently composer-in-residence, Karamu House, Cleveland. Recipient of Composer Award, National
Endowment for the Arts; received Rockefeller grant to study in Italy, grant from National
Endowment for the Arts to spend two months in Yaddo Artists Colony.

ANDERSON, THOMAS JEFFERSON. Composer, educator. Born August 17, 1928, Coatesville, Pa.
B. M. , West Virginia State College; M. M. E. , Pennsylvania State University; Ph. D. , University of Iowa. Composition teachers include T. Scott Huston, Phillip Bezanson, Darius
Milhaud. Held positions at West Virginia State College, Langston University, Tennessee
State University, Morehouse College. Chairman of music department at Tufts University,
1973-80. Honors and awards include MacDowell Colony Fellowship, Fromm Foundation
award, Coply Foundation award; composer-in-residence with the Atlanta Symphony Orchestra as result of grant from Rockefeller Foundation. Active as consultant-lecturer on
black music.

ARCHER, DUDLEY M. Organist, composer, teacher. Born October 1, 1899, Barbados, West Indies; died August 19, 1973, New York, N. Y. Studied at City College, New York City;
graduate of Guilmant Organ School, New York City. Associate of American Guild of Organists. Founder of Archer's Modern Music School, Brooklyn, N. Y. ; organist for 33
years at St. Augustine's Episcopal Church. In 1972 was Dean of Brooklyn Chapter of the
American Guild of Organists.

BAKER, DAVID N. Composer, cellist, educator. Born 1931, Indianapolis, Indiana. Received
B. Mus. and M. Mus. from Indiana University. Taught at Lincoln University (Mo.), Indiana Central College, and the Indianapolis public schools. Presently serves as head of the
jazz studies program, Indiana University. He had traveled extensively with Quincy Jones
and other famous jazz groups. Works have been commissioned by religious groups, including the Christian Theological Seminary, Catholic Music Educators Association, and a
Lutheran church. He is the author of several books on jazz improvisation.

BANKS, ROBERT. Pianist, organist, composer. Born 1930, Newark, N. J. Studied at Juilliard
School of Music and Montclair State Teachers College. Taught in Newark public schools.

BILLUPS, KENNETH BROWN. Music educator, composer, arranger, conductor, director. Born

131

1918. B.M., Lincoln University (Mo.); M.M., Northwestern University; postgraduate study, Northwestern University, Washington University (St. Louis). Director, Wings Over Jordan Choir, 1945-49; choirmaster in several churches in St. Louis. Chairman, music department, Sumner High School; founder and director of Legend Singers; member of faculty, University of Missouri; past president, National Association of Negro Musicians, 1963-68. Guest Conductor of Windsor Canada Symphony, Atlanta Festival Orchestra, St. Louis Symphony.

BOATNER, EDWARD H. Composer, arranger, conductor, teacher. Born November 13, 1898, New Orleans. Attended Chicago College of Music, New England Conservatory, and Boston Conservatory; studied composition with Louis Victor Saar, Felix Deyo, and Rudolph Schramm. Pioneer in research and development of Afro-American music. Director of Music for National Baptist Convention, 1926-32; devised a Comprehension Music Chart and book for piano students; author of pictorial work about outstanding Afro-Americans; wrote The Story of the Spirituals, a music book of the origin of 35 Afro-American slave spirituals. Has studio in New York City. Spiritual arrangements for solo voice have been sung by Marian Anderson, Roland Hayes, Paul Robeson, Leontyne Price, George Shirley, and many others.

BONDS, MARGARET. Pianist, composer. Born March 13, 1913, Chicago, Ill.; died April 26, 1970, Los Angeles. B.M.S., M.M., Northwestern University; studied at Juilliard School of Music. Awarded the Rosenwald Fellowship, Wanamaker Award, Roy Harris Scholarship. Toured as pianist. Best known for solo and choral arrangements. Wrote stage background scores "Shakespeare in Harlem," "U.S.A."

BURLEIGH, HARRY THACKER. Singer, composer, arranger. Born 1866, Erie, Pa.; died September 12, 1949, Stamford, Conn. Studied with Rubin Goldmark, Anton Dvorak, John White, Max Spicker; scholarship in voice to National Conservatory of Music, New York City. Concertized in Europe and United States; baritone soloist, St. George's Episcopal Church, New York City. Composed more than 90 songs; composed or arranged more than 50 choral compositions. Won Spingarn Achievement Medal; honorary M.M. degree, Atlanta University; honorary Doctor of Music degree, Howard University, Washington, D.C.

CARTER, ROLAND. Educator, composer, arranger. Born May 4, 1942, Chattanooga, Tenn. B.A., Hampton Institute; M.A., New York University; doctoral candidate, New York University. Present position, Director of Choirs, Hampton Institute, Director of Peninsula Youth Orchestra. Publishes with his own company, Mar-vel Music.

CHILDS, JOHN MICHAEL. Composer. Born October 4, 1932, Baltimore. Studied at the Juilliard School of Music and privately with Lee Hoiby. Worked with the Harkness School of Ballet, Alvin Ailey Dance Theatre, Jones-Haywood School of Ballet (Washington, D.C.).

CLARK, ROGIE EDGAR. Singer, composer, arranger. Born April 14, 1917. B.A., Clark College (Atlanta); M.A., Columbia University. Further study at Chicago Musical College, Juilliard School of Music. Received Ford Foundation grant, John Whitney Fellowship. Chairman of music department, Fort Valley State College (Ga.); Director of Harlem Recreation Center in New York City.

CLARY, SALONE. Music educator, pianist, composer. Born Portsmouth, Va. B.A. in Music Education, Norfolk State College. Present position, music teacher and organist in Norfolk.

COLEMAN, CHARLES D. Composer, organist. Born 1926, Detroit. B.M. and M.M., Wayne State University. Associate of American Guild of Organists (with honor). Studied with Virgil Fox, Van Dessel, and Walter Poole. Member of American Guild of Organists.

COOKE, CHARLES L. Born 1891, Louisville, Ky.; died 1958. B. M., M. M., D. M. A., Chicago
    Musical College. Staff arranger with Radio City Music Hall and music publishing teams
    in Detroit.

COOPER, WILLIAM B. Organist, choir director, composer. Born Philadelphia. B. M., M. M.,
    Philadelphia Musical Academy. Held positions at Hampton Institute, Lincoln University
    (Pa.), Bennett College (N. C.). Presently teaching at Wadleigh Intermediate School (New
    York City). Has held a number of positions as church organist, including present posi-
    tion at St. Martin's Episcopal Church (New York City). Member of American Guild of
    Organists. Owner of Dangerfield Music Co.

CUNNINGHAM, ARTHUR. Composer, conductor, author, bassist. Born November 11, 1928, Nyack,
    N. Y. B. A., Fisk University; studied at Juilliard School of Music; M. A., Teachers Col-
    lege, Columbia University; studied at Metropolitan Music School with Wallingford Riegger,
    Mekegan, Teddy Wilson. Wrote stage scores for "The Beauty Part" and "Violetta"; has
    written many compositions for all media, including over 400 popular songs; has written for
    television, musicals.

CURTIS, MARVIN V. Composer, choir director. Born February 12, 1951, Chicago, Ill. B. M. E.,
    North Park College; M. A., Presbyterian School of Education, Richmond, Va. Director of
    Church School Music, Riverside Church, New York City; founder and director of Riverside
    Community Chorale; choral director, Emmanuel Baptist Church, New York City.

Da COSTA, NOEL G. Violinist, composer, educator. Born December 4, 1929, Lagos, Nigeria;
    moved to West Indies at age of three; moved to New York City eight years later. B. A.
    in music, Queens College (New York City); M. A. (theory, composition), Columbia Univer-
    sity, where he received the Seidl Fellowship in composition; studied with Dallapiccola in
    Florence, Italy, on Fulbright Fellowship. Taught for two years at Hampton Institute (Va.);
    present position, Associate Professor of Music, Rutgers University. Conductor of the
    Triad Chorale; vice-president of the Society of Black Composers.

DAVIS, ELMER L., Sr. Conductor, teacher, composer, arranger. B. A., Langston University;
    M. M. E. (voice), University of Oklahoma. Organizer and conductor of The Chorus of
    Angels, which has given more than 450 performances; has performed often as soloist.
    Present position, Supervisor of Vocal Music, Tulsa (Okla.) Public Schools.

DAWSON, WILLIAM LEVI. Composer, conductor, arranger, trombonist, educator. Born 1898,
    Annestown, Ala. Studied at Harner Institute of Fine Arts, Kansas City, graduated with
    honors in composition; M. A. (composition and orchestration), Chicago Musical College;
    M. A., American Conservatory of Music; won Wanamaker Contest, 1930. Chairman of
    department of music, Tuskegee Institute; conductor of the famous Tuskegee Choir; retired
    in 1955. In great demand as guest conductor and lecturer. Works include compositions
    for orchestra, piano, chamber groups; best known for choral compositions and arrange-
    ments using the Negro spiritual.

De PAUR, LEONARD. Conductor, composer, arranger, lecturer, writer. Born 1915, Summit, N. J.
    Educated at University of Colorado, Juilliard School of Music, Columbia University,
    L'Universite Laval; private study with Henry Cowell, Hall Johnson, Pierre Monteux.
    Created and conducted the De Paur Chorus in more than 2, 300 performances between
    1947 and 1968; has recorded more than 20 albums; published choral series by Lawson-
    Gould Music and many others. Active in TV, radio, films, and theater. Present posi-
    tion, Director of Community Relations, Lincoln Center for the Performing Arts.

DETT, ROBERT NATHANIEL. Composer, arranger, pianist, conductor, music educator. Born

October 11, 1882, Drummondville, Ont.; died 1943.   B.M., Oberlin Conservatory; studied at American Conservatory of Music; Columbia University; University of Pennsylvania; Harvard University.   Taught at Lane College, Lincoln Institute (Mo.).   Director of Music at Hampton Institute (1913-31).   Directed the Hampton Institute Choir, which achieved international fame.   Taught at Sam Houston College, Bennett College.   A prolific composer and arranger of works based on the Negro folksong.   Won the Bowdoin Prize, Harvard University, for essay "The Emancipation of Negro Music"; Frances Bout prize for composition; and Harmon Foundation award for composition.   Best known for piano and choral works.

DITON, CARL R.   Pianist, composer, teacher.   Born 1886, Philadelphia; died 1969.   Studied at the University of Pennsylvania and in Germany; first Negro concert pianist to tour the U.S.   Director of music at Paine College and Talladega College.

DUNCAN, JOHN.   Educator, composer.   Born November 25, 1913, Lee County, Ala.; died September 15, 1975, Montgomery, Ala.   Earned music degrees from Temple University; studied at New York University.   Taught for 26 years at Alabama State University.

FAX, MARK.   Composer, music educator, organist.   Born 1911, Baltimore; died January 2, 1974, Washington, D.C.   B.M. (piano), Syracuse University; M.M. (composition), Eastman School of Music; Fellow, American Guild of Organists.   Taught at Paine College.   In the School of Music at Howard University he was Professor of Composition and held positions as Chairman of applied music department, Assistant to Dean of the College of Fine Arts, Acting Dean of College of Fine Arts (1970-72), and Director of School of Music (1972-74).   For 20 years he served as Minister of Music, Asbury Methodist Church.   He was a prolific composer whose works include three operas and many choral, vocal, and instrumental works.

FURMAN, JAMES.   Composer, choral conductor, educator.   Born 1937, Louisville, Ky.   B.M.Ed., M.Mus., University of Louisville; further study, Brandeis University, Harvard University.   Conductor-arranger-pianist for first Army Show (1961); has held a number of positions as choirmaster and organist; taught in the public schools of Louisville.   Presently, Assistant Professor of Music, choral director, Western Connecticut College.

GILLUM, RUTH HELEN.   Music educator, pianist, composer, arranger, and conductor.   Born 1907, St. Louis.   B.Mus. (piano), M.M. (piano), University of Kansas; graduate study, Indiana University.   Chairman of music department at Prairie View State College; Philander Smith College; North Carolina Central University, 1944-71.

GREGORY, PERCY.   Pianist, educator.   Born Washington, D.C.   B.Mus. and M.M., Howard University.   Studied composition with Mark Fax and Russell Woollen.   Doctoral candidate (piano and composition), University of Maryland.   Has taught in the public schools of the District of Columbia.   Present position, Associate Professor of Music, University of the District of Columbia; also serves as associate conductor of the University Chorale.

HAILSTORK, ADOLPHUS C., III.   Composer, educator.   Born 1941, Rochester, N.Y.   B.Mus., Howard University; M.M., Manhattan School of Music; Ph.D. (composition), Michigan State University (East Lansing).   Held teaching position at Youngstown State University; presently Associate Professor and composer-in-residence, Norfolk State University.   Received Lucy E. Moton Fellowship from Howard University to study with Nadia Boulanger in Paris.   "Celebration" for orchestra commissioned by J. C. Penney for "Bicentennial Gift to the Nation" (1976).   Received National Band Association Award, 1977; "Spiritual" commissioned by Edward Tarr for brass ensemble.

HAIRSTON, JACQUELINE BUTLER.   Educator, composer, arranger.   Born Charlotte, N.C.   B.M.E.,

Howard University; M.A., Columbia University; studied at Juilliard School of Music. Taught for many years at Johnson C. Smith University (Charlotte, N.C.); choir director/organist for churches in Charlotte, N.C. Present position, North Peralta Community College, Oakland, Calif.

HAIRSTON, JESTER. Composer, arranger, conductor, actor, author. Born July 9, 1901, North Carolina. B.A., Tufts University (music theory), Juilliard School. Assistant conductor to Hall Johnson, 15 years; trained choirs for radio and Broadway musicals; organized choir in 1943; arranged and conducted background music for Duel in the Sun, Portrait of Jenny, Friendly Persuasion. Actor in film and television. In great demand as lecturer and choral clinician; toured Europe in 1961 and 1963 for State Department to teach American folksongs; in 1965, 1966, and 1968 sent to West Africa as a goodwill ambassador by State Department.

HALL, FREDERICK DOUGLASS. Music educator, conductor, arranger, composer, author. Born December 14, 1898, Atlanta. Studied at Morehouse College; Chicago Musical Institute; Teachers College, Columbia University; Royal College of Music. Director of Music at Clark College, Morris Brown College, Alabama State College, Dillard University.

HANCOCK, EUGENE WILSON (WHITE). Organist, composer. Born 1929, St. Louis. B.M., University of Detroit; M.M., University of Michigan; S.M.D., Union Theological Seminary. Member, American Guild of Organists; served as organist and choirmaster in Detroit and New York City. Present position, Associate Professor of Music, Manhattan Community College, New York City; organist and director, St. Phillip's Episcopal Church, New York City.

HANDY, WILLIAM CHRISTOPHER. Composer, arranger, bandmaster, cornetist, publisher, often called Father of the Blues. Born November 16, 1873, Florence, Ala.; died March 29, 1958, New York City. Taught briefly at Teachers' A&M College for Negroes (Huntsville, Ala.). Cornetist in Mahara's Minstrels. Organized and conducted his own dance band; wrote the first blues composition, "Memphis Blues." In addition to the blues, wrote piano, voice, and choral works; edited collections of blues and spirituals. Wrote autobiography, Father of the Blues.

HARRIS, ROBERT A. Composer, conductor, music educator. Born 1938, Detroit. B.A. (Music Education) and M.A. in Music, Wayne State University; Ph.D. (composition), Michigan State University. Taught vocal and choral music in Detroit; was Associate Professor and Director of Choral Activities, Michigan State University (East Lansing); presently Director of Choral Activities, Northwestern University.

HICKS, ROY EDWARD. Composer, music educator, conductor, arranger. Born January 14, 1931. B.A., Paul Quinn College; M.A., Prairie View A&M University. Further study at North Texas State University; Southern Methodist University; candidate for D.M.A. in church music, Southwest Baptist Theological Seminary. Teacher of the Year--1970, Dallas, Tex.; one of "10 Outstanding New Composers of 1973." Present position (since 1970) organist, choir director, department head, Tuskegee Institute.

JAMES, WILLIS LAURENCE. Music educator, violinist, musicologist, arranger, composer. Born 1909, Montgomery, Ala.; died December 29, 1966. Degrees from Morehouse College and Chicago Musical College, in composition; Rosenwald and Carnegie Fellowships; authority on development of Afro-American music. Consultant to Institute of Jazz Studies, New York City; taught at Alabama State Teachers College, Fort Valley State College, and Spelman College.

JESSYE, EVA. Composer, arranger, conductor. Born January 20, 1895, Coffeyville, Kans. Studied at Wilberforce University; M.A., Allen University; honorary M.A., Wilberforce University; honorary doctorate, Allen University. Organized and conducted the first all-black choir, which toured the United States; choral director of Porgy and Bess productions, 1935-58; Lost in the Stars; Four Saints in Three Acts; choral director for Hallelujah. Arranged and published many works performed by her group, The Eva Jessye Choir.

JOHNSON, HALL. Conductor, composer, arranger, violinist. Born March 12, 1888, Athens, Ga.; died April 30, 1970, New York City. Studied at Atlanta University, Knoxville Institute, Hahn School of Music, Institute of Musical Arts. Formed famous Hall Johnson Choir in 1925; toured the United States and Europe in 1951; music director of Broadway production Green Pastures; wrote score for Run, Little Chillun. Best known for his arrangements of Negro spirituals. Received two Holstein Prizes for compositions (1925, 1927), Harmon Award (1931), honorary doctorate from Philadelphia Musical Academy.

JOHNSON, J. ROSAMOND. Composer. Born 1873, Jacksonville, Fla.; died 1954. Studied at the New England Conservatory of Music. Collaborated with his brother, James Weldon Johnson, to write many songs; also teamed with Robert Cole to write show tunes and popular music. Toured Europe and America performing spirituals and excerpts from Porgy and Bess.

KAY, ULYSSES. Composer. Born 1917, Tucson, Ariz. M.A., University of Arizona; Eastman School of Music (composition); studied with Paul Hindemith at Yale University, composition at Columbia University. Awarded the Julius Rosenwald Fellowship, Prix de Rome, Guggenheim Fellowship. Music consultant for Broadcast Music, Inc. A prolific composer who has written 20 works for full orchestra, works for string orchestra, chorus, piano, and organ.

KERR, THOMAS H., Jr. Pianist, composer, educator. Born 1915, Baltimore. B.Mus. (piano and theory), M.Mus., Eastman School of Music, University of Rochester. Awarded prize in composition from Composers and Authors of America; received the Rosenwald Fellowship in Creative Music. Appeared as piano soloist with the National Symphony Orchestra, Washington, D.C., at the National Art Gallery and Phillip's Gallery (Washington, D.C.). For many years was organist/choir director at Plymouth Congregational Church. Professor Emeritus, Howard University.

KING, BETTY JACKSON. Music educator, conductor, composer. B.M. (piano), M.M. (composition), Roosevelt University. Held positions in Chicago at Jacksonian Community Center, University of Chicago Laboratory School, Roosevelt University; and at Dillard University.

LOGAN, WENDELL. Composer, educator. Born 1940, Thomson, Ga. M.Mus., Southern Illinois University; Ph.D., State University of Iowa. Held positions at Florida A&M, Ball State University; presently on faculty of Oberlin Conservatory.

McLIN, LENA. Composer, arranger, music educator. Chairman of Kenwood High School music department, Chicago; in demand as lecturer, clinician because of her interest in developing a new form of music, which she calls "art rock"; an innovative teacher who has popularized her totally unstructured approach to teaching music to young people.

MARGETSON, EDWARD HENRY. Organist, composer. Born December 31, 1891, British West Indies; died January 1962, New York City. Came to the U.S. in 1919. Studied at Columbia University with Daniel Gregory Mason and Seth Bingham. Associate of American Guild of Organists; awarded the Victor Bauer Fellowship and the Joseph Mozenthal Fellowship in composition at Columbia University; received Julius Rosenwald Award. Organizer and Director of the Schubert Society of New York; organist and choirmaster of the Church of the Crucifixion in New York City.

MAYES, ROBERT. Born St. Louis. B. Mus., Howard University. Entertainment director of special services, U. S. Army. Taught in Chicago public schools; pianist-arranger for many groups, including his own trio. Appeared with Walter Hawkins, James Cleveland, Albertina Walker. Present position, Minister of Music, Christ Universal Temple Ensemble, which performs weekly on a local radio station with minister-founder, Dr. Johnnie Coleman.

MELLS, HERBERT FRANKLIN. Pianist, music educator, composer. Born 1909, Darien, Ga.; died in 1953. B. S., Morehouse College; M. A., Indiana University; Ph. D., University of Iowa. Taught at Langston University; Hampton Institute; Chairman of music department, Tennessee State University (Nashville).

MERRIFIELD, NORMAN L. Composer, arranger, conductor, music educator. Born 1906, Louisville, Ky. B. M. and M. S. (music major), Northwestern University. Taught at Fisk University, Alabama State Teachers College, Florida A&M College; conductor of Army bands.

MONTAGUE, J. HAROLD. Music educator, conductor, arranger, composer. Born May 27, 1907; died April 29, 1950. B. M., Oberlin Conservatory; M. M., Syracuse University. Head of music department, South Carolina State College; Chairman of music department, Virginia State College (Petersburg); director of Virginia State College Choir.

MOORE, CARMAN. Composer, performer. Born 1936. Studied at Oberlin Conservatory; earned degree from Ohio State University; M. Mus., Juilliard School of Music. Lectures at Manhattan College, Yale University; is active as lecturer and writer. Served as president of the Society of Black Composers.

MOORE, DOROTHY RUDD. Composer, arranger, teacher. Born New Castle, Del. B. M. (composition), School of Music, Howard University; studied with Mark Fax (Howard University); Nadia Boulanger, Paris; Chou Wen-Chung, New York. Has written principally for instrumental ensembles. Taught at Harlem School of the Arts, New York University, Bronx Community College. Founder and former vice-president of Society of Black Composers.

MOORE, UNDINE SMITH. Music educator, composer, arranger. Born 1904, Jarratt, Va. B. S., Fisk University; M. A., Teachers College, Columbia University; advanced study at Eastman School of Music, Manhattan School of Music, and Fisk University with John Work. Associate Professor of Music; Chairman, department of music Theory and Composition; and Coordinator of Interdisciplinary Studies in Music and Art at Virginia State College, 1927-72; pianist, organist; lecturer at leading universities, here and abroad. Codirector of Black Music Center. Present position, Professor of Music Theory, Virginia Union University.

MORGAN, WILLIAM ASTOR (pseudonym, Jean Stor). Composer, piano and theory teacher. Born 1890; died Bronx, N. Y.

NICKERSON, CAMILLE. Pianist, composer, arranger, music educator. Born 1888, New Orleans. B. M., M. M., Oberlin Conservatory; studied at Juilliard School of Music; Teachers College, Columbia University. Began a brilliant teaching career in 1926 at Howard University School of Music; has done extensive research in Creole folk music of Louisiana; in great demand as lecturer and performer; received Rosenwald Fellowship.   Now retired and lives in Washington, D. C.

PARKER, REGINALD NATHANIEL, Sr.   Organist, teacher, composer, arranger.   Born 1929; died 1970.   B. M. (organ), Howard University; M. M. (composition), Manhattan School of Music; composition, School of Sacred Music, Union Theological Seminary (New York City).   Associate, American Guild of Organists; instructor of music, Norfolk State College and in Brooklyn, N. Y.; organist-choirmaster, Washington, D. C.; Norfolk, Va.; New York, N. Y.

PERKINSON, COLERIDGE-TAYLOR.   Composer, conductor.   Born 1932.   B. M., M. M. (composition), Manhattan School of Music.   Studied at Berkshire Music Center, Mozarteum, Netherlands Radio Union, Hilversum.   Assistant conductor of Dessoff Choirs, member of faculty of Manhattan School of Music; conductor, Brooklyn Community Symphony Orchestra; music director for the Symphony of the New World.   Has composed for radio, movies, television, and ballet.

PERRY, JULIA.   Composer, conductor.   Born 1927, Akron, Ohio; died 1979.   B. M., M. M., Westminster Choir School, Princeton, N. J.; further study at Juilliard School of Music, Berkshire Music Center; studied with Nadia Boulanger, Paris; Dallapiccola, Italy.   Has written instrumental and vocal music.

PITTMAN, EVELYN LaRUE.   Composer, educator.   Born 1910, McAlester, Okla.   B. A., Spelman College (Atlanta, Ga.); M. M., University of Oklahoma.   Taught in Oklahoma City.   Has written and arranged many choral compositions.

PRICE, FLORENCE B.   Composer, arranger, music educator.   Born 1888, Little Rock, Ark.; died 1953, Chicago.   Studied at New England Conservatory, Chicago Musical College, American Conservatory of Music.   Won Wanamaker Prize for composition; composer and arranger for instrumental and vocal music.

PRICE, JOHN E.   Composer, pianist, educator.   Born 1935, Tulsa, Okla.   Earned degree in composition and piano from Lincoln University (Mo.).   Joined staff of Karamu Theatre (Cleveland) as composer, pianist, and vocal coach.   For ten years Chairman of Music and Fine Arts, Florida Memorial College; host of radio program, "Classical Black"; present position, member of music faculty, Eastern Illinois University.   Has composed over 500 works.

REECE, CORTEZ DONALD.   Music educator, arranger, composer.   Born 1908, Guthrie, Okla.; died July 30, 1974, Los Angeles.   A. B., Fisk University; M. A., Ph. D., University of Southern California.   Taught at Langston University; head of music department and division of humanities, Bluefield State College (W. Va.) until retirement in 1973.

RIVERS, CLARENCE JOSEPH.   Priest of the Archdiocese of Cincinnati, composer, arranger, conductor.   Born 1931, Selma, Ala.   After ordination in 1956 taught English in high school for boys and was part-time assistant pastor; a pioneer in introducing Afro-American Culture into Catholic worship; popular as a lecturer, conductor, and clinician.   Founded Simuli, Inc. (music publishing company); consultant for the application of the performing arts and mixed-media presentations in the areas of education and celebrations.   In 1966 received gold medal from Catholic Art Association for "An American Mass Program."

ROBERTS, HOWARD A.   Conductor, singer, composer, arranger, teacher.   Studied at Baldwin-Wallace College, Western Reserve University; B. M., M. M., Cleveland Institute of Music.

Assistant Professor of Music, Morgan State College. Musical director, conductor/ arranger for Harry Belafonte, Leslie Uggams Show, Alvin Ailey American Dance Theatre, The Great White Hope, Trumpets of the Lord, Revelations, Donald McKayle Dance Company, and many others. Director of the Howard Roberts Chorale.

ROBINSON, ALPHONSE. Organist/director, now retired. Born 1910, East St. Louis, Ill. Studied at Philander Smith College (Little Rock, Ark.), St. Louis Music and Arts University, La Mont School of Music, Denver University. His choral work, "Soliloquy to a Martyred Hero," written in collaboration with Betty McConnell and Virgil V. Rosenberger, received world premiere at the Iliff School of Theology (Denver).

ROBINSON, JOSEPHUS. Composer, arranger, pianist. Born Augusta, Ga. Studied at Chicago College of Music (piano and theory); Gervin Institute (piano); B.M. (composition), Cosmopolitan School of Music (Chicago); M.M. (composition), Chicago Conservatory of Music. Taught theory and piano, AM&N College (Pine Bluff, Ark.). One of staff members for Singtime Music Publishers (Chicago); has written many arrangements of spirituals and gospel songs. Now lives in Chicago.

ROXBURY, RONALD. Composer. Born 1946, Fruitland, Md. Studied at Peabody Conservatory. Compositions include works for voice, flute, piano, and orchestra.

RYDER, NOAH FRANCIS. Composer, arranger, music educator. Born 1914, Nashville, Tenn.; died 1964, Norfolk, Va. B.S., Hampton Institute; M.M., University of Michigan. Taught in public schools of North Carolina, Palmer Memorial Institute (N.C.), Winston-Salem Teachers College, and Hampton Institute, where he also conducted the choir. Head of the music department of the Norfolk Division of Virginia State College. Best known for choral and vocal arrangements of Negro spirituals.

SIMPSON, EUGENE THAMON. Pianist, arranger, singer, educator. Born 1932, North Carolina. B. Mus., Howard University; B.M., M.M., Yale University; Ed.D., Columbia University. Held position on faculty of Virginia State College as choir director and teacher; served as Chairman of division of humanities, Bowie State College, also choir director; chairman of department of music, Glassboro State College, 1975-80; presently Professor of Music at this institution.

SMITH, HALE. Composer, arranger. Born 1925, Cleveland. B.M. (composition), Cleveland Institute of Music. Has served as music editor for Edwin B. Marks Music Corporations, Sam Fox Music Publishers. Associate Professor, University of Connecticut; Adjunct Associate Professor of Music, C. W. Post College of Long Island University. Has written extensively for orchestra and instrumental ensembles and is well known as a jazz composer and arranger. Works have been performed by Cincinnati Orchestra, Cleveland Orchestra, Symphony of the New World, and Louisville Orchestra.

SMITH, WILLIAM HENRY. Born 1908; died 1944. Native of Massachusetts. Musical training in Boston and Chicago. Directed music at Olivet Baptist Church in Chicago.

SOUTHALL, MITCHELL BERNARD. Pianist, composer, arranger, conductor. Born August 30, 1922, Rochester, N.Y. Studied at Langston University, University of Iowa, Oklahoma College of Liberal Arts. Chairman of music department and choir director at Langston University, Lane College, Texas College; Professor of Music Theory and Piano, Rust College. Has composed choral and piano works.

STILL, WILLIAM GRANT. Often called Dean of Negro Composers, lecturer. Born May 11, 1895,

Woodville, Miss.; died 1978.   Educated at Wilberforce University and Oberlin Conservatory of Music; private study with George W. Chadwick and Edgard Varèse.   Orchestrated for W. C. Handy, Willard Robinson, Paul Whiteman, Artie Shaw, Don Voorhees.   Has conducted major symphony orchestras.   Received the Guggenheim and Rosenwald Fellowships; honorary degrees from Wilberforce University, Howard University, Oberlin College, and Bates College.   Has received numerous awards and citations for his compositions and contributions to American music; important commissions include Columbia Broadcasting System, New York World's Fair (1939-40), League of Composers, and the Cleveland Orchestra.

STOR, JEAN (See MORGAN, WILLIAM ASTOR)

SWANSON, HOWARD.   Composer.   Born 1909 Atlanta; died 1978.   Educated at Cleveland Institute of Music (composition); won Rosenwald Fellowship; studied with Nadia Boulanger in France; received grant from Academy of Arts and Letters; awarded Guggenheim Fellowship.   Best known for orchestral works and songs.   Short Symphony performed by New York Philharmonic under Mitropoulos; this work was judged by New York Critics Circle to be the best orchestral work played during 1950-51.

TAYLOR, MAUDE B. CUMMINGS.   Organist, composer.   Born Bermuda.   Studied at Columbia University; Matlock College, England; American Conservatoire, Fontainebleau, France.   Music studio, Brooklyn, N.Y.; organist, Cornerstone Baptist Church, Brooklyn.

TILLIS, FREDERICK.   Educator, composer.   Born Galveston, Tex.   B.A., Wiley College (Texas); M.A., Ph.D., University of Iowa.   Served as head of music department, Kentucky State College; taught at Wiley College, Grambling College.   Directed 356th U.S. Air Force Band.   Present position, Professor of Music, University of Massachusetts.

WALKER, GEORGE THEOPHILUS.   Composer, pianist, educator.   Born 1922, Washington, D.C.; earned degree from Oberlin College; artist diploma in piano and composition, Curtis Institute, where he studied with Rudolf Serkin and Gian-Carlo Menotti; D.M.A., Eastman School of Music.   Concertized for several years as pianist under management of National Concert Artists and Columbia Artists.   Received many fellowships, prizes, and awards, including the Fulbright, Guggenheim, MacDowell Colony, and Whitney Fellowships, and the Rockefeller Foundation Grant.   Taught at the New School for Social Research, Smith College, and the University of Colorado.   Present position, Chairman of the department of music, Rutgers University.

WHALUM, WENDELL PHILLIPS.   Conductor, pianist, educator, composer, arranger.   Born Memphis, Tenn.   B.A., Morehouse College; M.A., Columbia University; Ph.D., University of Iowa.   Chairman of department of music, Morehouse College, conductor of well-known Morehouse Male Choir.   Prepared chorus for premiere performance of Treemonisha, by Scott Joplin; has prepared other choruses for performances with the Atlanta Symphony Orchestra, Robert Shaw, conductor.   Has written several articles on some aspect of Afro-American music; has recorded three volumes of arrangements of spirituals.   Toured Africa with choir under sponsorship of the State Department.

WHITE, CLARENCE CAMERON.   Violinist, composer, arranger, music educator.   Born August 10, 1880, Clarksville, Tenn.; died June 30, 1960, New York City.   Studied at Oberlin College; studied violin with Zacharewitch and composition with Samuel Coleridge-Taylor in London.   In 1924 appointed head of music department, West Virginia State College; 1934, Director of Music, Hampton Institute.   Organized community music programs for National Recreation Association; received David Bispham Award for opera, Oranga; Harmon Foundation Award.

WILLIAMS, ARNOLD K. Music educator, conductor, composer. Born February 19, 1928, Chicago. B. S., M. S. (music education), University of Illinois. Supervisor of Music Education and Art Coordinator, Gary (Ind.) Public Schools. Active as director of church choirs, clinician, and conductor of bands and orchestras.

WILLIAMS, JULIUS P., Jr. Conductor, educator, composer. Born 1954. B. S. (Mus. Ed.), M. M. E., Hartt School of Music. Received grant from the American Society of Composers, Authors and Publishers (1979-80, 1980-81) for compositions in musical theater. Presently on faculty of Hartt School of Music; Visiting Fellow in Music and Afro-American studies at Wesleyan University.

WILSON, OLLY. Composer, bass violist. Born 1937, St. Louis. B. Mus., Washington University; M. Mus., University of Illinois; Ph. D., University of Iowa. Awarded first prize in International Electronic Music Competition held at Dartmouth College. Has held positions at Florida A&M University, West Virginia University, Oberlin Conservatory of Music, and the University of California (Berkeley). His works are widely heard and represent a variety of media.

WORK, JOHN WESLEY III. Composer, arranger, music educator, author. Born June 15, 1901, Tilahome, Tenn.; died 1967, Nashville, Tenn. B. A., Fisk University; B. A., Columbia University; M. A., Yale University; M. B., Juilliard School of Music. Chairman of music department, Fisk University; director of internationally known Fisk Jubilee Singers. Best known for research in field of Negro folksong and for choral and vocal works. Compiled "American Negro Songs."

APPENDIXES

Appendix A: SELECTED SOURCE READINGS

I. Books and Dissertations

Alho, Olli. The Religion of the Slaves: A Study of the Religious Tradition and Behaviour of Plantation Slaves in the U. S. 1830-1865. Helsinki: Academia Scientiarum Fennica, 1976.

Allen, William Francis. Slave Songs of the United States. New York: A. Simpson, 1867. Republished, Oak, 1967.

Allison, Roland Lewis. "Classification of the Vocal Works of Harry T. Burleigh (1866-1949) and
Some Suggestions for Their Use in Teaching Diction in Singing. " Ph. D. dissertation, Indiana
University, 1966.

Arvey, Verna. Studies of Contemporary Composers: William Grant Still. New York: J. Fischer,
1939.

Baker, David N. , Lida M. Belt, and Herman C. Hudson, eds. The Black Composer Speaks. Metuchen, N. J. : Scarecrow, 1978.

Berry, Lemuel, Jr. Biographical Dictionary of Black Musicians and Music Educators, Vol. 1.
Guthrie, Okla. : Educational Book, 1978.

Brawley, Benjamin. Negro Builders and Heroes. Chapel Hill: University of North Carolina Press,
1937.

Brooks, Tilford. "A Historical Study of Black Music and Selected 20th Century Black Composers. "
Ed. D. dissertation, Washington University, 1972.

Butcher, Margaret J. The Negro in America. New York: Arno, 1968.

Butcher, Vada E. Development of Materials for a One-Year Course in African Music for the General Undergraduate Student. Washington, D. C. : Howard University, Center for Ethnic Music,
1970.

_____. Annual Report. Washington, D. C. : Howard University, Center for Ethnic Music, 1971.

Courlander, Harold. Negro Folk Music, U. S. A. New York: Columbia University Press, 1963.

143

De Lerma, Dominique-Rene. Black Music in Our Culture. Kent, Ohio: Kent State University Press, 1970.

_____. Reflections on Afro-American Music. Kent, Ohio: Kent State University Press, 1973.

Du Bois, William Edward Burghardt. The Soul of Black Folk. Chicago: McClurg, 1903.

Evans, Arthur L. "The Development of the Negro Spiritual as Choral Art Music by Afro-American Composers with an Annotated Guide to the Performance of Selected Spirituals." Ph. D. dissertation, University of Miami, 1972.

Fisher, Miles Mark. Negro Slave Songs. New York: Cornell University Press, 1953.

Frazier, E. Franklin. The Negro Church in America. New York: Schocken, 1963.

Garcia, William B. "The Life and Choral Music of John Work (1901-1967)." Ph. D. dissertation, University of Iowa, 1973.

Hare, Maude Cuney. Negro Musicians and Their Music. Washington, D. C.: Associated Publishers, 1963. Reprint ed., New York: Da Capo, 1974.

Harris, Carl G. "A Study of Characteristic Trends Found in the Choral Works of a Selected Group of Afro-American Composers and Arrangers." D. M. A. dissertation, University of Missouri, Kansas City, 1972.

Hayes, Roland. My Songs. Boston: Little, Brown, 1948.

Hughes, Langston. Famous Negro Music Makers. New York: Dodd, Mead, 1955.

Jackson-Brown, Irene. Afro-American Religious Music: A Bibliography and a Catalogue of Gospel Music. Westport, Conn.: Greenwood, 1979.

Johnson, J. Rosamond, and J. Weldon Johnson. The Book of American Negro Spirituals. New York: Viking, 1925.

Johnson, Marjorie S. "Noah Francis Ryder (1914-1964): A Study of His Life, Works, and Contribution to Music Education." Master's thesis, Catholic University of America, 1968.

Katz, Bernard, ed. The Social Implications of Early Negro Music in the United States. New York: Arno and the New York Times, 1969.

Krehbiel, Henry Edward. Afro-American Folksongs. New York: Schirmer, 1914. Republished, New York: Ungar, 1962.

Levine, Lawrence W. Black Culture and Black Consciousness: Afro-American Folk Thought from Slavery to Freedom. London: Oxford University Press, 1977.

Levy, Eugene. James Weldon Johnson: Black Leader, Black Voice. Chicago: University of Chicago Press, 1973.

Locke, Alain LeRoy. The Negro and His Music. Washington, D. C.: Associates in Negro Folk Education, 1936.

_____. Negro Art: Past and Present. New York: Arno and the New York Times, 1969 (rpt).

Lovell, John. Black Song: The Forge and the Flame. New York: Macmillan, 1972.

McBrier, Vivian Flagg. R. Nathaniel Dett: His Life and Works. Washington, D. C.: Associated, 1977.

Marsh, J. B. T. The Story of the Jubilee Singers; With Their Songs. Boston: Houghton, Mifflin, 1881. Reprint ed., New York: Negro University Press, 1969.

Merritt, Nancy G.   "Negro Spirituals in American Collections: A Handbook for Students Studying Negro Spirituals. "   Master's thesis, Howard University, 1940.

Odum, Howard W. , and Guy B. Johnson.   The Negro and His Songs.   Chapel Hill: University of North Carolina Press, 1925.

Roach, Hildred.   Black American Music: Past and Present.   Boston: Crescendo, 1973.

Rublowsky, John.   Black Music in America.   New York: Basic, 1971.

Southern, Eileen.   The Music of Black Americans: A History.   New York: Norton, 1971.

_____.   Readings in Black American Music.   New York: Norton, 1971.

Thompson, Leon E.   "A Historical and Stylistic Analysis of the Music of William Grant Still and a Thematic Catalogue of His Work. "   D. M. A. dissertation, University of Southern California, 1967.

Thurman, Howard.   Deep River and the Negro Speaks of Life and Death.   Richmond, Ind. :   Friends United Press, 1975.

Trotter, James M.   Music and Some Highly Musical People.   Boston: Lee and Shepard, 1881. Reprint ed. , Johnson Reprint Corp. , 1968.

Work, John Wesley, and Frederick J. Work.   Folk Songs of the American Negro.   Nashville, Tenn. : Work Brothers, 1901.

Work, John Wesley, Sr.   Folk Songs of the American Negro.   Nashville, Tenn. :   Fisk University Press, 1915.   Reprint ed. , New York: Negro University Press, 1969.

II.   Articles

"A Birthday Offering to William Grant Still. "   The Black Perspective in Music, May 1975, Vol. 3.

Brooks, Tilford.   "The Black Musician in American Society, "   Music Journal, 1975, 40-45.

Burlin, Natalie Curtis.   "The Negro's Contribution to the Music of America, "   The Craftsman, 1925.

Caldwell, Hansonia.   "Conversation with Hale Smith: A Man of Many Parts, "   The Black Perspective in Music, Spring 1975, 59-76.

Dett, R. Nathaniel.   "The Emancipation of Negro Music, "   The Southern Workman, April 1918, 172-176.

Garcia, William.   "Church Music, "   The Black Perspective in Music, Fall 1974, 145-157.

Hayes, Roland.   "Music of Aframerica: My Songs, "   Music Journal, February 1963, 20, 82-83.

Hunt, Joseph.   "Conversations with Thomas J. Anderson, "   The Black Perspective in Music, Fall 1973, 157-165.

Jackson, Barbara Garvey.   "Florence Price, Composer, "   The Black Perspective in Music, Spring 1977, 31-43.

Jackson-Brown, Irene V.   "Afro-American Song in the 19th Century: A Neglected Source, "   The Black Perspective in Music, Spring 1976, 22-38.

James, Willis Laurence.   "The Romance of the Negro Folk Cry in America, "   Phylon, Vol. XVI, No. 1.

McGinty, Doris E.   "Conversations with Camille Nickerson: The Louisiana Lady," The Black Perspective in Music, Spring 1979, 81-94.

Margetson, Edward.   "Folk Music," The Southern Workman, 1927, 487-492.

Maultsby, Portia K.   "Black Spirituals: An Analysis of Textual Forms and Structures," The Black Perspective in Music, Spring 1976, 54-69.

Murray, Charlotte W.   "The Story of Harry T. Burleigh," The Papers of the Hymn Society, No. 4, October 1966.

Simpson, Eugene Thamon.   "The Hall Johnson Legacy," The Choral Journal, January 1971.

Southall, Geneva.   "Black Composers and Religious Music," The Black Perspective in Music, Spring 1974, 45-50.

Southern, Eileen.   "Conversations with Olly Wilson: The Education of a Composer," Part I, The Black Perspective in Music, Spring 1977, 90-103.

_____.   "Conversations with Olly Wilson: The Education of a Composer," Part II, The Black Perspective in Music, Spring 1978, 57-70.

Whalum, Wendell P.   "James Weldon Johnson's Theories of Performance Practices of Afro-American Folksongs," Phylon (Special J. W. Johnson Centennial Issue), December 1971.

_____.   "Black Hymnody," Review and Expositer, Summer 1973.

_____.   "The Spiritual As Mature Choral Composition," Black World, July 1974.

Work, John W.   "Changing Patterns in Negro Folk Songs," Journal of American Folklore, April-June 1949 (reprint of a paper delivered at the nineteenth annual Fisk Festival of Music and Arts, Nashville, Tenn., April 29-May 1, 1948).

_____.   "The Negro Spiritual," The Papers of the Hymn Society, September 1961.

Appendix B: SELECTED DISCOGRAPHY

BRIGHAM YOUNG UNIVERSITY A CAPPELLA CHOIR
   Ralph Woodward, Director

   Welcome Yule - Ulysses Kay
   College Choirs at Christmas; The Classics Record Library; Book of the Month Club, Inc.;
   10-5573

BURLEIGH, HARRY T.

   O Lord, Have Mercy On Me.   Illinois Wesleyan University Collegiate Choir; David Nott,
   conductor.   Recorded Publications Corporation cc - 8

   Spirituals.   Victor 1799
                       1966
                       2032
                       4371
                       8959
                       20793

101114
C-27
M-554

CHRIST UNIVERSAL TEMPLE ENSEMBLE (Chicago)
Robert Mayes, Director

Featuring Della Reese. CUT 60619

Tower of Power.

DAWSON, WILLIAM L.

I Couldn't Hear Nobody Pray. C. W. Post College Chorus and Chamber Singers. Sound Rec-Golden Crest CCS 8050 1977

Mary Had a Baby. Yale University Choir; J. Somary, conductor. Carillon Records LP-101

Out in the Fields. Oakland Youth Symphony Orchestra. Desto 7107

Soon Ah Will Be Done. De Paur Infantry Chorus; Leonard De Paur, conductor. Columbia AL-45

Soon Ah Will Be Done. Brank Krsmanovich Chorus of Yugoslavia. Monitor MP-576

Soon Ah Will Be Done. Roger Wagner Chorale. Capital P-8431

Spirituals. Victor 4556

De PAUR, LEONARD.

All 'Round de Glory Manger; O Po' Little Jesus. Masterworks CL 923

Danse Calinda; Pauline, Pauline. De Paur Chorus; Leonard De Paur, conductor. Mercury SR 90418

Nobody Knows de Trouble I See. Columbia AL 45

Swing Low, Sweet Chariot. De Paur Infantry Chorus; Leonard De Paur, conductor. Columbia AL 45

DETT, R. NATHANIEL.

The Chariot Jubilee. Morgan State College Choir; Nathan Carter, conductor. Audio House AHR 30F75

Listen to the Lambs. Mormon Tabernacle Choir. Philips NBL-5012

The Ordering of Moses. The Eastman Singers; David Fetler, conductor. Eastman Festival of American Music, 1960

The Ordering of Moses. Talladega College Choir; William Dawson, conductor. Mobile Symphony Orchestra, Silver Crest TAL-428685

Spirituals. Victor M-879

FISK JUBILEE SINGERS

> Bright, Bright Star.   Hall Johnson Choir.   ERA 20012
>
> Folkways Records.   Fisk Jubilee Singers; John W. Work, director.   FA 2372
>
> "Little David Play on Your Harp."   Adele Addison and the Jubilee Singers; Mrs. James A. Myers, director.   KAPP:KL 1109, 1959

HAIRSTON, JESTER.

> Jester Hairston and His Chorus: A Profile of Negro Life in Song.   Murbo Records MLP 6000
>
> In dat Great Gettin' Up Mornin'.   De Paur Infantry Chorus; Leonard De Paur, conductor. Columbia AL-45

HOWARD UNIVERSITY CHOIR
Warner Lawson, Director

> Spirituals.   RCA Victor LM-2126
>
> Spirituals.   The Spoken Word of Howard Thurman; Thomas H. Kerr, Jr., organist. Howard University

HOWARD UNIVERSITY CHOIR
J. Weldon Norris, conductor

> Spirituals.   Howard University, 1980

HOWARD UNIVERSITY CHOIR ALUMNI
Evelyn White, Director

> Warner Lawson Memorial Concert (1972).   Mark MC 8357

JOHNSON, J. WELDON

> God's Trombones.   Montclair Gospel Chorale; Saffel Huggs, conductor.   United Artists UAL 4039

KAY, ULYSSES

> Choral Triptych.   King's Chapel Choir of Boston; Cambridge Festival Strings; Daniel Pinkham, conductor.   Cambridge CRM-416
>
> How Stands the Glass Around?   Randolph Singers; David Randolph, conductor.   Composers Recording, CRI-102
>
> Two Folksong Settings: Sally Anne; Blow, Ye Winds.   Leonard De Paur and Chorus. Commissioned by J. C. Penney Project
>
> What's in a Name.   Randolph Singers; David Randolph, conductor.   Composers Recording, CRI-102

KNOXVILLE COLLEGE CONCERT CHOIR
Nathan Carter, Conductor

Spirituals. Inauguration Special. Century Records 28936

LOGAN, WENDELL

Songs of Our Time. Ball State University Chorus and Instrumental Ensemble; Golden
Crest S-4087

MOORE, UNDINE

Lord We Give Thanks to Thee. Virginia Union Choir; Odell Hobbs, conductor. Easter
Recording ERS (Wayside Drive, Richmond, VA 23255)

MOREHOUSE COLLEGE GLEE CLUB
Wendell Whalum, Conductor

Vol. I (1968)
Vol. II (1970)
Vol. III (1972)
Vol. IV (1974)
Vol. V (1977)
Vol. VI (1979) Hughes Set - Wendell Logan

Morehouse College (Atlanta, GA 30314)

MORGAN STATE UNIVERSITY CHOIR
Nathan Carter, Conductor

Welcome Yule! - Ulysses Kay
Go Tell It on the Mountain - Thomas H. Kerr, Jr.
A Babe Is Born - George Walker
Carillon Heigh-Ho - Julia Perry
Mary Had a Baby - Hall Johnson
Come, Thou Long-Expected Jesus - James Furman

College Choirs at Christmas; The Classics Record Library; Book of the Month Club, Inc.
10-5573

Black Composers--Music of Praise

Wasn't That a Mighty Day? - John Work
Mary, Mary, Where Is Your Baby? - Jester Hairston
Go Tell It on the Mountain - Thomas H. Kerr, Jr.
A Babe Is Born - George Walker
Carillon Heigh-Ho - Julia Perry
Silent Night - Thomas H. Kerr, Jr.
Mary Had a Baby - Hall Johnson
Come Thou Long-Expected Jesus - James Furman
In His Care-O - William L. Dawson
Out in the Fields - William L. Dawson
O Praise the Lord - George Walker
Sing unto the Lord - George Walker
Precious Lord, by Thomas Dorsey - Nathan Carter
Psalm I - Nathan Carter

Music of Early Black Composers
ACDA Live Concert; St. Louis, Missouri
March 6, 1975

Requiem, excerpts - Jose Mauricio Nunes-Garcia
The Chariot Jubilee - R. Nathaniel Dett
Sahdji, excerpts - William Grant Still
The Evening Star - Coleridge-Taylor
Ring de Christmas Bells - Jester Hairston
Sinner, Please Don't Let This Harvest Pass - J. Harold Montague

Excerpts from A Concert of Sacred Music in Classical/Jazz/Rock/Gospel Styles.
MENC/NAJE Concert; Atlanta, Georgia

Lord, Have Mercy; Apostles' Creed; from "The Brotherhood of Man Mass" - Clarence
Joseph Rivers.   Crest Records ME-72-19

Black Composers Series Vol. 7
London Symphony Orchestra; Paul Freeman, conductor.

Sahdji (Ballet for Orchestra and Chorus) - William Grant Still
Lyric for Strings - George Walker

Columbia Records M33433

OBERLIN COLLEGE CHOIR
    Robert Fountain, Director

Psalm 23; In Memoriam, Martin Luther King, Jr. - Olly Wilson
Recordings, Series 1, Vol. 19

PERKINSON, COLERIDGE-TAYLOR

Fredome-Freedom. King's Chapel Choir of Boston; Cambridge Festival Strings; Daniel
Pinkham, conductor.   Cambridge CRM-416

ROBERT SHAW CHORALE
    Robert Shaw, Conductor

Deep River and Other Spirituals

Every Time I Feel the Spirit - William Dawson
This Ol' Hammer - John Work
This Little Light o' Mine - John Work
Who Is That Yonder - Howard Boatner
There Is a Balm in Gilead - William Dawson
Soon-a Will Be Done - William Dawson
My Lord, What a Morning - William Dawson
Ain'a That Good News - William Dawson

RCA LSC-2247

I'm Goin' to Sing; 16 spirituals
RCA Victor LM 2580

ROBERTS, HOWARD

Let My People Go. Howard Roberts Chorale; Howard Roberts, conductor.   Columbia
MS 7189

SMITH, HALE

>In Memoriam--Beryl Rubinstein; Kulas Choir and Chamber Orchestra; Robert Shaw, con-
>ductor. Composers Recordings Inc. CRI SD-182

STILL, WILLIAM GRANT

>Sahdji. Eastman School Chorus; Eastman-Rochester Symphony Orchestra; Howard Hanson,
>conductor. Mercury SR-90257

TUSKEGEE INSTITUTE CHOIR
William L. Dawson, Conductor

>Spirituals. Westminister Records WGM 8154.

UTAH STATE UNIVERSITY CHORALE
William Ramsey, Director

>Concert with Jester Hairston
>
>Gossip, Gossip
>What Kind o' Shoes You Gonna Wear?
>Uncle Johnny's Mule
>Mary, Mary, Where Is Your Baby?
>Swing a Lady Gum-pum
>Ha'nted House
>Poor Man Lazrus
>Sakura, Sakura
>Home in Dat Rock
>Goodbye Song

VIRGINIA STATE COLLEGE CHOIR
Eugene Thamon Simpson, Director

>Hall Johnson Song Book
>Black Heritage Series, Vol. I
>
>Cert'n'y Lord
>I've Been 'Buked
>Lord, I Don't Feel No-ways Tired
>When I Was Sinkin' Down
>His Name So Sweet
>Fix Me, Jesus
>Honor, Honor
>Run Li'l Chillun
>I'll Never Turn Back
>I Couldn't Hear Nobody Pray
>Elijah Rock
>City Called Heaven
>Ain't Got Time to Die
>
>William Dawson Song Book
>Black Heritage Series, Vol. II
>
>Every Time I Feel the Spirit
>Mary Had a Baby
>King Jesus Is A-Listening

Talk About a Child That Do Love Jesus
There Is a Balm in Gilead
Li'tl Boy Child
Oh What a Beautiful City
Ain't That Good News
Hail Mary
Jesus Walked This Lonesome Valley
Soon Ah Will Be Done
Behold the Star
Ezekiel Saw de Wheel

VIRGINIA STATE COLLEGE CONCERT CHOIR
Carl Harris, Jr., Conductor

Undine Smith Moore Song Book
Afro-American Heritage Series, Vol. III

I Just Come from the Fountain
Let Us Make Man in Our Image
Hail Warrior
The Lamb
Striving After God
Daniel, Daniel, Servant of the Lord
Bound for Canaan's Land
Sinner You Can't Walk My Path
Fare You Well
Lord, We Give Thanks to Thee
Children Don't Get Wary
Plenty Good Room

VIRGINIA UNION UNIVERSITY CHOIR
Odell Hobbs, Director

O What a Beautiful City - William Dawson
Hail Warrior - Undine Moore
I Want to Be Ready - William Dawson
Whatsoever a Man Soweth - Mark Fax
In His Care-O - William Dawson
Sanctus - Lena McLin
God Is Alright - Robert Mayes
I Got a Robe - arr. Odell Hobbs
Let Us Break Bread Together - Noah Ryder

EVELYN WHITE CHORALE
Evelyn White, Director

Choral Music of Black Composers

A Shining Light (from the Opera Til Victory Is Won) - Mark Fax
Ave Maria - Ronald Roxbury
Glory to God - Robert Harris
Kyrie - Robert Harris
Make a Joyful Noise - Reginald Parker
Listen to the Lambs - R. Nathaniel Dett
Were You There - Harry T. Burleigh
Plen'y Good Room - Thomas H. Kerr, Jr.
I'll Never Turn Back - Hall Johnson
City Called Heav'n - Hall Johnson
'Way Over in Beulah Lan' - Hall Johnson

WILSON, OLLY

In Memoriam, Martin Luther King, Jr. Oberlin College Choir; Robert Fountain, conductor. Recordings Series 1, Vol. 19

WORK, JOHN W., III

Black Folk Song Arrangements in Jubilee Day Centennial Anniversary Concert. Fisk Jubilee Singers; Matthew Kennedy, conductor. Afro-American Music Opportunities Association. Minneapolis. January 1972

Go Tell It on the Mountain. Harry Simeone Singers; Harry Simeone, conductor. Diplomat Stereo XS-1021 (Best Loved Christmas Carols)

Go Tell It on the Mountain. RCA Victor Chorale; Robert Shaw, conductor. RCA Victor LP 1112 (Christmas Carols)

Go Tell It on the Mountain. Manhattan Concert Chorale. Galliard Recordings GM 101. (A Galaxy of Yuletide Music)

Isaac Watts Contemplates the Cross. Broadman Records X TBV 83031-445-33589

Is a Light a Shining in the Heavens? Peabody College Madrigalians; Irving Wolf, conductor. Album Series 305

The Joys of Mary. Harvard Glee Club; G. Wallace Woodworth, conductor. CRS 411 (Christmas Carols in Cambridge)

My Lord What a Morning. Harvard Glee Club; Elliot Forbes, conductor. Carillon Records LP 122-M08P-3770. (Songs of the World)

My Lord, What a Mornin'. Combined Choirs--1st International Choral Festival; G. Wallace Woodworth, conductor. RCA Red Label LSC 7043

Po' Ol Laz'rus. Yale Glee Club; Marshall Bartholomew, conductor. Columbia 796-36463

The Singers. Centennial Celebration of Fisk University (1866-1966); Fisk University Choir; Members of Nashville Symphony Orchestra; April 28, 1966. Century Records

Spiritual Arrangements. Fisk Jubilee Singers; John W. Work, conductor. Word Rec W-LP4007

This Light of Mine. Robert Shaw Chorale; Robert Shaw, conductor. RCA-L.M. 2274 (Deep River and Other Spirituals)

This Light of Mine. Rust College Choir with Leontyne Price; L. U. Holmes, conductor. RCA LSC-3183

CATALOG OF SELECTED VOICE OF AMERICA RECORDINGS

Washington Broadcasting Service
U.S. Information Agency

(Recorded Sound Division)

Library of Congress
Washington, D.C.

A: COLLEGE CHOIRS

ATLANTA-MOREHOUSE-SPELMAN COLLEGE CHOIR
Kemper Harreld, Conductor

Jesus, lay your head in the window Let us break bread together There is a balm in Gilead The rocks and the mountain	F. 16	6828
Beautiful Savior The rocks and the mountain shall all flee away There is a balm in Gilead Daniel saw the stone Great day the righteous marching Song of the angels	Program 34	OM 5324 DS-685
Lost in the night I wonder as I wander/Appalachian Folksong We are climbing Jacob's ladder King Jesus is a-listening	Program 38	OM 5331 DS-689
Swing low, sweet chariot See four and twenty elders Send down the spirit Wheels a-turning in my heart Return, redeemer beloved Study war no more His name so sweet	Program 21	OM 5487 DS-137

BETHUNE-COOKMAN NEGRO COLLEGE CHOIR
Daytona, Florida
Alzeda C. Hacker, Director

Set down servant Let us break bread together Steal away I couldn't hear nobody pray	F. 5	6710 VOA 324

FAYETTEVILLE STATE TEACHERS CHOIR
Fayetteville, North Carolina
George van Hoy Collins, Conductor

My soul just ain't contented We're travelling to the grave Gwine up Don't you weep no more Mary Gonna journey away Rock in Jerusalem You better mind	Program 24	OM 5163 DS-215
Son of Mary King of Kings There's a meeting here tonight In that great gettin' up morning Steal away	Program 27	
Come to me Rock in Jerusalem	Program 36	OM 5330 DS-687

Better be ready
Now the day is over
Sky so bright
Stand still, Jordan

FISK UNIVERSITY CHOIR
Nashville, Tennessee
John F. Ohl, Director

He is King of Kings	F. 15	6828
Keep me from sinking down		VOA-419/418
Roll, Jordan roll		
Study war no more		
Soon in the morning		

FLORIDA A&M COLLEGE CHOIR
J. Harrison Thomas, Conductor

My way is cloudy	Program 31	OM 5165
Cheer the weary traveller		DS-313
Golden slippers		
I'll never turn back no more		
I wish I was in heaven settin' down		
Swing low, sweet chariot		

HAMPTON INSTITUTE CHOIR
Hampton, Virginia
Henry F. Switten, Director

Don't you weep no more Mary	F. 17	VOA 439/420
Let us cheer the weary traveller		
There is a balm in Gilead		
Set down servant		
Go tell it on the mountain	F. 18	VOA 440/441
Wade in the water		
Children come on home		
Peter, go ring them bells		

HOWARD UNIVERSITY CHOIR
Warner Lawson, Director

Go tell it on the mountain	Program 28	ncp 847
My Lord what a morning		DS-303
Shouts (Ring dem bells)		
Jesus lay your head in the window		
Live-a humble		

NORTH CAROLINA COLLEGE CHOIR
James E. Dorsey, Conductor

Soon I will be done	Program 23	OM 5163
Study war no more		DS-214
As by the streams of Babylon		
Roll Jordan roll		
My God is so high		
In bright mansions above		

On my journey	Program 35	OM 5330
I'm so glad trouble don't last always		DS-868
Oh wasn't that a wide river		
Hear little angels singing		
I'll never turn back no more		
Tone the bells		

ST. AUGUSTINE COLLEGE CHOIR
    T. Curtiss Mayo, Director

Ain't that good news	Program 26	ncp 846
Deep river		DS-301
Dig my grave		
I'll never turn back		
O' what a beautiful city		
I wonder as I wander (American folksong)		

SHAW UNIVERSITY CHOIR
    Raleigh, North Carolina
    Harry G. Smith, Director

Climbing up the mountain children	F. 21	6829
Wasn't that a mighty day		VOA 353/354
Soon I will be done		

TALLADEGA COLLEGE CHOIR
    Talladega, Alabama
    Frank Harrison, Director

I want to climb Jacob's ladder	F. 6	6710
He never said a mumbling work		VOA 325
I know the Lord has laid his hands on me		
Walk together children		

TUSKEGEE INSTITUTE CHOIR
    Tuskegee, Alabama
    William L. Dawson, Director

Theme - Deep River	Program 1	ncp 1176
Oh my good Lord show me the way		17-3646
Deep river		
Ain'-a that good news		
Ain't gonna study war no more		
Everytime I feel the spirit		
Rise and shine	F. 19	6853
Were you there when they crucified my Lord?		VOA 441/440
Egypt land		
Swing low, sweet chariot		

WILEY COLLEGE CHOIR
    Marshall, Texas
    Gilbert Allen, Director

Amen	F. 22	6829
Sinner, please don't let this harvest pass		VOA 354/353

Medley: a) Fix me Jesus
            b) I've been 'buked
When I was sinkin' down

WILLISTON SCHOOL CHOIR
Wilmington, North Carolina

Theme - Deep River	Program 17	ncp 1362	
Rock in Jerusalem		17-4260	
Ride on, King Jesus			
I'll never turn back no more			
King of Kings			
My soul couldn't be contented			

XAVIER UNIVERSITY CHOIR
New Orleans, Louisiana
Clifford Richter, Director

Ezekiel saw de wheel	F. 23	VOA 355/380
Soon I will be done		
When I was sinkin' down		
Ain'-a that good news		

MISCELLANEOUS COLLEGE CHOIRS

F. 7   6725
               VOA 407/408

Going home to live with God (Soon I will be done)
    Livingstone College Choir; Salisbury, N. C.; Myron
    Thomas, director

King Jesus is a-listening; Lincoln University Glee Club;
    Lincoln, Pa.; Orin C. Southern, Director

In-a my heart; Livingston College Choir

Joshua fit de battle of Jericho; Lincoln University Glee Club

Hand me down; Livingston College Choir

B: OTHER CHOIRS

HALL JOHNSON CHOIR
Hall Johnson, Director

Ain't got time to die	F. 8	6725
I'm going down that lonesome road		VOA 408/407
Have you got good religion (Cert'ny Lord)		
I couldn't hear nobody pray		
Deep river		

WINGS OVER JORDAN CHOIR
Glynn T. Settle, Director

Theme - Deep River	Program 2	ncp 1175

Climbin' up the mountain, chillun   17-3647
Wade in the water   9455-2
Rock-a my soul
Walk together, chillun
Ride on King Jesus
You know, Lord

Theme - Deep River   Program 13   839
Trampin'   17-4177
Show me the way   5664-1
Sometimes I feel like a motherless child
Didn't it rain
Trying to get ready
When the saints go marching in

Theme - Deep River   Program 18   ncp 1362
Where shall I be when the first trumpet sounds   17-4261
I'm troubled
Trying to get ready to try on my long white robe
Run, sinner, run

Something   Program 39   ncp 1349
O, my good Lord   DS-946
Somebody touched me
Take me to the water
You must have that true religion
The old ship of Zion
Trying to get ready

I'm on my way   Program 41   OM 5435
I want to be ready   DS-948
I'm gonna wait till the day is done
We shall walk through the valley
I'm troubled
I'm working on the building
Don't you get weary
The Lord will provide

Didn't my Lord deliver Daniel   Program 43   OM 5503
I'm bound to leave this world   DS-1044
In the year of Jubilee
Get on board, little children
Amen
When the saints go marching in
Through the storm
The heavenly Father

Trampin'   Program 50   OM 5602
Everytime I feel the spirit   DS-1244
Stand by me
Wheel in the middle of the wheel
Keep me from sinking down
Just a closer walk with thee

Please search my heart   Program 58   OM 6088
Bye and bye   DS-1994
Want to go to heaven when I die
I want to cross over to see my Lord
'Tis the old ship of Zion
When the saints go marching in

Little David play on your harp My soul is a witness for my Lord Somebody touched me I am leaning on the Lord Please search my heart You must have that true religion	F. 4	ncp 878 OM 6521
Standing in the need of prayer New-born again There must be a God somewhere Does anybody here know my Jesus He'll understand and say "well done" Give away, Jordan	F. 9	6711 VOA 409
Oh, what a beautiful city I want to die easy when I die Where shall I be when the 1st trumpet sounds I've got a home in that rock, don't you see? #3 Rock my soul	F. 13	VOA 417 6969
Same train carried my mother I'm going to die with that staff on my hand There's plenty good room I'm troubled Let me ride	F. 20	6853 VOA 352/353
You can tell the world about this It's my desire Don't stay away I must keep a'movering' along	F. 24	6830 VOA 380/381

CAMP MEETING CHOIR
J. Garfield Wilson, Director

Theme - Deep River On the way heaven Plenty good room Until you die Joshua fit the battle of Jericho What a beautiful city Go feed the spirit Along the river Jordan	839	17-4182
Theme - Deep River Hand me down my silver trumpet No hiding place That rocky land My Lord, what shall I do When I rise I want my crown		17-4251
Theme - Deep River Judgement day is comin' 'round What you goin' to wear? Sometimes I feel like a motherless child Little David play on your harp The key to the kingdom Let me fly		17-4252
You've got to stand	846	DS 300

Something within me
In that morning
Ride on, King Jesus
Nobody knows the trouble I see
Look away

There must a Lawd somewhere	OM 5165	DS-314
Couldn't hear nobody pray		
Lord, I just got over		
I'm just a poor wayfaring stranger		
I'm willing to bear my burden		
Since I laid my burden down		
Does anybody hear		

I'm gonna walk with Thee	OM-5538	DS-1046
Been in the storm so long		
Want to go to heaven		
I'm standin' on that rockin' air		
All over this world		
Death came a-creepin'		
Climbin' up the mountain		

Shepherd go feed my sheep	OM 6045	DS-1990
Down by the river of Jordan		
He did my God wrong		
Standin' in the need of prayer		
My Lord, what a morning		
I got a home in that rock		
Great day		

Religion is a fortune	F 1.	OM 6486
I want to die easy		
One morning soon		
I'm singing, all my records will be there		
Steal away		
I won't mind		

I'm gonna walk right in an' make myself at home	F 2.	OM 6486
I'm waiting for my savior		
Ring dem golden bells		
Lord, we're almost home		
We're going home to heaven		
Hand me down my silver trumpet		

Great day, the righteous marching	F 3.	ncp 878
I'm trying to get ready		
Since I laid my burden down		
There's a cross for everyone		
My Lord, what a morning		
Well, anyhow, I'm on my way to heaven		

I'm waiting for my saviour	F 12.	6827
I've won my crown		
We want to join the band		
I'm leaning on the Lord		
He's all and all		
He got lost in the storm		

Judgement day is comin'	F 14.	6959
Just a closer walk with thee		
Lord, what shall I do		

Been in the storm so long
Want to go to heaven
King Jesus is a rock in a weary land

While I'm down here prayin' Lead me on Don't wander 'bout home Reign, Massa Jesus, reign On my way to heaven, anyhow	F 25.	6960

CHARIOT WHEELS CHOIR
Lawrence Mann, Director

Hold on Oh Mary, don't you weep Nobody knows the trouble I've seen Music in the mine I am seeking for a city	F 10.	6771
Write my name He answers me The holly and the ivy (Christmas carol) Until I reach my home I want Jesus to walk with me	OM 5331	DS-688
Singing with a sword in my hand Walk, Mary, down the lane Go down, Moses Something within Set down, servant Prayer is the key to heaven		
He that believeth I am seeking for a city Your God and mine Praise to the Lord Soft and tenderly	ncp 1349	DS-947
Noah and the ark You better run Hold the wind Open the window Didn't it rain Ain't you glad Battle Hymn of the Republic	OM 5435	DS-949
On my journey home Hush, somebody's callin' my name Oh, Mary, don't you weep I want two wings to fly away Wait till I get on the road Blow your trumpet, Gabriel	OM 5503	DS-1045
I will lift up mine eyes Oh, John When I reach that city To see that ship sail by I got a home up in that kingdom Hallelujah I've been down in the sea Shout for joy	OM 5538	DS-1047

Rock in Jerusalem	OM 5602	DS-1243
Ain't you glad you got good religion?		
That heavenly light		
When I reach that city over there		
Jesus, lay your head in the window		
You better mind		

Hold the wind, don't let it blow	OM 5647	DS-1245
There's no hidin' place down here		
Hard trials		
Sinner, please don't let this harvest pass		
Just Jesus		
I know the lord laid his hands on me		

Good news, chariot's coming	OM 6045	DS-1989
All over this world		
City called heaven		
Ain't you glad		
Wait'til I put on my robe		

New born again	OM 6181	DS-1991
I'll never turn back no more (Dett)		
Old Zion's children marching along		
He's got the whole world in his hand		
Wade in the water children		
Blow your trumpet Gabriel		

Hand me down	OM 6181	DS-1992
Just a closer walk with thee		
Rain Salvation		
There's a cross for everyone		
I'm on my way to heaven		
Well anyhow		

Rise, shine the light is a coming	OM 6088	DS-1994
Witness for my Lord		
Remember now thy creator		
Heaven bells		
So wide		
Shines like the morning star		

I'm new born again	OM 6403	DS-2521
Come down angels		
He's got his eyes on you		
Salvation is free		
Done paid my vow to the Lord		

That religion that my Lord give me	OM 6411	DS-2522
Wade in the water children		
What kind of shoes are you going to wear?		
Lord, I want to be a christian		
Dry bones		
I want to go to heaven		

When the turn comes along	OM 6411	DS-2523
I been 'buked		
I couldn't hear nobody pray		
Oh, poor little Jesus		
Heaven, heaven		
When the saints go marching in		

LEGEND SINGERS
    Kenneth Phillips, Conductor

        Sunday morning band   845
        We are climbing Jacob's ladder
        Wade in the water, little chillun
        Run, sinner, run
        I know de Lawd
        Let it shine
        Noah built the ark

SIDELIA SINGERS
    Rufus A. Brent, Conductor

        Good news, Christ's coming   1363   DS-147
        I couldn't hear nobody pray
        Rise, shine, the light is a-coming
        Ezekiel saw the wheel
        Tramping
        Every time I feel the spirit

METROPOLITAN A CAPELLA CHOIR
    Joseph Polk, Conductor

        Hush, somebody's callin' my name   845   DS-304
        There's no hiding place down here
        We shall walk through the valley
        I'll be a servant
        Listen to the lambs

        Climbing up the mountain children   4801   DS-136
        The old ship of Zion
        Set down, servant
        Trouble in the air
        Let me ride
        So glad
        Judgement day is rolling around

NORTHERN CALIFORNIA CHORUS
    Elmer Keedon, Director

        Brother Henry   OM 5582   DS-1186
        Rock-a my soul
        John, the revelator
        My Lord's arriving
        Riding in the chariot
        Peter on the seas

        Shout hallelujah   OM 5582   DS-1187
        Reign, Massa Jesus, reign
        Amen
        I stood on the river Jordan
        Shortenin' bread

Appendix C: ADDRESSES OF MUSIC PUBLISHERS
              AND COMPOSERS OF UNPUBLISHED WORKS

Leslie Adams
9409 Kemptom Avenue
Cleveland, OH 44108

American Composers Alliance
170 West 74th Street
New York, NY 10023

Associated Music Publishers
866 Third Avenue
New York, NY 10022

Augsburg Publishing House
426 South Fifth Street
Minneapolis, MN 55415

David N. Baker
Indiana University
Bloomington, IN 47401

Belwin-Mills Publishing Corp.
25 Deshon Drive
Melville, NY 11746

Birchard Music Co.
(See Summy-Birchard Co.)

Boatner Associates
76 West 69th Street
New York, NY 10023

Joseph Boonin, Inc.
(See European American Music Distributors
     Corp.)

Boosey and Hawkes, Inc.
P. O. Box 130
Oceanside, NY 11572

Boston Music Co.
116 Boylston Street
Boston, MA 02116

Bourne Co.
1212 Avenue of the Americas
New York, NY 10036

Broadman Press
127 Ninth Street North
Nashville, TN 37203

Broude Brothers, Ltd.
56 West 45th Street
New York, NY 10036

Chappell and Co. , Inc.
609 Fifth Avenue
New York, NY 10017

John Childs
128 Lafayette Avenue
Brooklyn, NY 11238

Choral Art Publications
(See Sam Fox Publishing Co.)

John Church Music Co.
(See Theodore Presser)

Franco-Colombo
(See Belwin-Mills Publishing Corp.)

William B. Cooper
61 Manhattan Avenue
White Plains, NY 10607

Marvin Curtis
277 Washington Avenue
Brooklyn, NY 11205

Noel da Costa
Rutgers University
Newark, NJ 07102

Dangerfield Music Co.
61 Manhattan Avenue
White Plains, NY 10607

D'Laniger Music Co.
915 Druid Circle
Norfolk, VA 23504

Duchess Music Corp.
(See Belwin-Mills Publishing Corp.)

John Duncan
(order from Dorothy Duncan Shepherd)
3418 East 104th Street
Kansas City, MO 64137

Elkan-Vogel Co. , Inc.
(See Theodore Presser Co.)

European American Music Distributors Corpora-
     tion
195 Allwood
Clifton, NJ 07012

Mark Fax
(Order from Mrs. Dorothey Fax)
6405 Sixteenth Street, N. W.
Washington, DC 20012

Carl Fischer, Inc.
62 Cooper Square
New York, NY 10003

J. Fischer and Bros.
(See Belwin-Mills Publishing Corp.)

Mark Foster Music Co.
Box 4012
Champaign, IL 61820

Sam Fox Publishing Co.
1540 Broadway
New York, NY 10036

Frank Music Corp.
119 West 57th Street
New York, NY 10019

James Furman
Western Connecticut State College
181 White Street
Danbury, CT 06810

Galaxy Music Corporation
2121 Broadway
New York, NY 10023

Gemini Press
c/o Alexander Broude
1619 Broadway
New York, NY 10019

General Music Publishing Co.
(See Boston Music Co.)

General Words and Music
(See Neil A. Kjos Music Co.)

H. W. Gray, Inc.
(See Belwin-Mills Publishing Corp.)

Percy Gregory
University of District of Columbia
Music Department
916 G Street, N. W.
Washington, DC 20004

Adolphus C. Hailstork
Norfolk State College
Norfolk, VA 23504

Hammon Music Co.
(See Boatner Associates)

Eugene Hancock
204 West 134th Street
New York, NY 10030

Handy Brothers
200 West 72nd Street
New York, NY 10023

Robert A. Harris
Northwestern University
School of Music
Evanston, IL 60201

Hinshaw Music Co.
P. O. Box 470
Chapel Hill, NC 27514

Holt, Rinehart and Winston, Inc.
383 Madison Avenue
New York, NY 10017

Hope Publishing Co.
380 South Main Place
Carol Stream, IL 60187

Ralph Jusko Music Co.
c/o Willis Music Co.
7380 Industrial Road
Florence, KY 41042

Thomas H. Kerr, Jr.
P. O. Box 681
Howard University
Washington, DC 20059

Neil A. Kjos Music Co.
525 Bussee Highway
Park Ridge, IL 60068

Lawson-Gould Music Publishers
(See G. Schirmer, Inc.)

Leeds Music Co.
(See Belwin-Mills Publishing Corp.)

Hal Leonard Publishing Corp.
960 East Mark Street
Winona, MN 55987

Wendell Logan
Oberlin College
Box 31
Oberlin, OH 44074

MCA Music
(See Belwin-Mills Publishing Corp.)

McAfee Music Corp.
c/o Lorenz Publishing Co.
501 East Third Street
Dayton, OH 45401

Edwin B. Marks
(See Belwin-Mills Publishing Corp.)

Mar-vel Music Co.
P. O. Box 6411
Hampton, VA 23668

Robert Mayes
Christ Universal Temple
8601 South State Street
Chicago, IL 60619

Mercury Music Corp.
(See Theodore Presser Co.)

Music 70 Music Publishers
170 North-East 33rd Street
Fort Lauderdale, FL 33334

Mutual Music Society
(See Chappell and Co., Inc.)

New Valley Music Press
Sage Hall 21
Smith College
Northampton, MA 01060

Northwestern School of Music Press
2436 West Grand Boulevard
Detroit, MI 48208

Oxford University Press
200 Madison Avenue
New York, NY 10016

J. A. Parks Co.
(See Neil A. Kjos Music Co.)

Peer International Corp.
1619 Broadway
New York, NY 10019

Pembroke Music Co.
(See Carl Fischer, Inc.)

C. F. Peters Corp.
373 Park Avenue South
New York, NY 10016

Piedmont Music Co.
(See Belwin-Mills Publishing Corp.)

Plymouth Music Co., Inc.
17 West 60th Street
New York, NY 10023

Theodore Presser Co.
Presser Place
Bryn Mawr, PA 19010

Pro Art Publications
469 Union Avenue
Westbury, NY 11590

Remick Music Corp.
(See Warner Bros. Music Publications)

Richmond Music Press
P.O. Box 465
Richmond, IN 47374

G. Ricordi
(See Belwin-Mills Publishing Corp.)

J. J. Robbins
c/o Music Sales
33 West 60th Street
New York, NY 10023

Alphonse Robinson
2744 Gaylord Street
Denver, CO 80205

Josephus Robinson
7704 South Honore Street
Chicago, IL 60620

Rodeheaver-Hall Mark Co.
c/o Word Inc.
P.O. Box 1970
Waco, TX 76703

R. D. Row Music Co.
(See Carl Fischer, Inc.)

Rudmor Publishing Co.
33 Riverside Drive
New York, NY 10023

E. C. Schirmer Music Co.
112 South Street
Boston, MA 02111

G. Schirmer, Inc.
866 Third Avenue
New York, NY 10022

Schmitt, Hall and McCreary Co.
110 North Fifth Street
Minneapolis, MN 55403)

Schuman Music Co.
(See Bourne, Inc.)

Shawnee Press Inc.
Delaware Gap, PA 18327

Skidmore Music Publications
(See Plymouth Music Co.)

Slave Ship Press
5030 Northwest Seventh Avenue
Miami, FL 33127

Southern Music Publishing Co., Inc.
1619 Broadway
New York, NY 10019

Standard Music Publications
P.O. Box 1043, Whitman Square
Turnerville, NJ 08012

Summy-Birchard Co.
1834 Ridge Avenue
Evanston, IL 60204

Stimuli Inc.
15 West Sixth Street
Cincinnati, OH 45202

Frederick C. Tillis
Department of Music and Dance
University of Massachusetts at Amhearst
Amhearst, MA 01002

Tosci Music Corp.
(See Belwin-Mills Publishing Corp.)

Volkein Brothers, Inc.
117 Sandusky Street
Pittsburgh, PA 15212

Walton Music Corp.
17 West 60th Street
New York, NY 10023

Warner Bros. Music Publications
75 Rockefeller Plaza
New York, NY 10019

Weintraub Music Co.
33 West 60th Street
New York, NY 10023

M. Witmark and Sons
(See Warner Bros. Music Publications)

Henry A. Williams
G. P. O. Box 2055
New York, NY 10001